The Philosophy of Henry Thoreau

Also available from Bloomsbury

Aesthetics, Arts, and Politics in a Global World, by Daniel Herwitz
Aesthetic Theory, Abstract Art, and Lawrence Carroll, by David Carrier
The Aesthetic Illusion in Literature and the Arts, edited by Tomáš Koblížek
The Philosophy and Art of Wang Guangyi, edited by Tiziana Andina and Erica Onnis
The Philosophy of Susanne Langer, by Adrienne Dengerink Chaplin

The Philosophy of Henry Thoreau

Ethics, Politics, and Nature

Lester H. Hunt

BLOOMSBURY ACADEMIC
LONDON • NEW YORK • OXFORD • NEW DELHI • SYDNEY

BLOOMSBURY ACADEMIC
Bloomsbury Publishing Plc
50 Bedford Square, London, WC1B 3DP, UK
1385 Broadway, New York, NY 10018, USA
29 Earlsfort Terrace, Dublin 2, Ireland

BLOOMSBURY, BLOOMSBURY ACADEMIC and the Diana logo are trademarks of
Bloomsbury Publishing Plc

First published in Great Britain 2020
This paperback edition published in 2021

Copyright © Lester H. Hunt, 2020

Lester H. Hunt has asserted his right under the Copyright, Designs and Patents Act, 1988, to be identified as Author of this work.

For legal purposes the Acknowledgments on p. xii constitute an extension of this copyright page.

Cover image: Circa 1850: Henry David Thoreau (1817–1862) © Hulton Archive / Stringer / Getty Images

All rights reserved. No part of this publication may be reproduced or transmitted in any form or by any means, electronic or mechanical, including photocopying, recording, or any information storage or retrieval system, without prior permission in writing from the publishers.

Bloomsbury Publishing Plc does not have any control over, or responsibility for, any third-party websites referred to or in this book. All internet addresses given in this book were correct at the time of going to press. The author and publisher regret any inconvenience caused if addresses have changed or sites have ceased to exist, but can accept no responsibility for any such changes.

A catalogue record for this book is available from the British Library.

A catalog record for this book is available from the Library of Congress.

ISBN: HB: 978-1-3500-7902-1
PB: 978-1-3502-5402-2
ePDF: 978-1-3500-7903-8
eBook: 978-1-3500-7904-5

Typeset by Newgen KnowledgeWorks Pvt. Ltd., Chennai, India

To find out more about our authors and books visit www.bloomsbury.com and sign up for our newsletters.

In Memoriam
Stanley Louis Cavell
1926–2018

To the states or any one of them, or any city of the states,
 Resist much, obey little,
Once unquestioning obedience, once fully enslaved . . . .
Walt Whitman, *"To the States"*

Contents

Preface (Which Is Meant to Be Read)	ix
Acknowledgments	xii
A Note on Citations	xiii

I Context: His Life and Times 1
   1. His Life 1
   2. His Times 9
II Politics and the Logic of *Walden* 15
   1. The Argument of "Civil Disobedience" 15
   2. What *Walden* Is 17
   3. Proof and Necessity 22
   4. Proof and Possibility 28
   5. Thoreau's Vitalism 32
   6. Philanthropy versus Virtue 36
   7. "Civil Disobedience" in the Context of *Walden* 45
III Knowing Right from Wrong 49
   1. The Voice of Conscience 49
   2. Assessing Thoreau's Intuitionism 56
   3. Two Ways of Relying on Intuition 64
   4. The Problem of John Brown 71
   5. The Idea of the Neighbor in *Walden* 74
IV Economy 77
   1. A Problem: Nature and Asceticism 77
   2. The Curse of Trade 78
   3. Higher Laws and Lower 80
   4. How Good Things Become Bad 85
   5. Exchange-Avoidance 87
   6. Thoreauvian Economy 90
   7. Critique of Commerce 92
   8. Another Response to Thoreau's Challenge 95
   9. Relevant Benefits of Commerce 99
   10. One Problem Solved 108

V Nature 111
   1. Wilderness and Wildness 111
   2. The Nature of Nature 122
   3. The Sacred Neighbor 127
   4. Environmental Policy 136

Appendix: Analogical Argument 141
Notes 149
Bibliography 159
Index 163

Preface (Which Is Meant to Be Read)

This little book is a personal one, as I think any book about Thoreau should be. The first time I read *Walden* I was living alone beside a pond in the woods. When the head came off my ax, I reattached it by following the method of doing so that Thoreau describes in chapter I (which involves slipping the handle back into the head and soaking it in the pond). I also tried the recipe for making bread without leavening that he quotes from his beloved Marcus Portius Cato. (It tasted much as I imagine a cedar roofing shingle would taste.) More importantly, I was at that time very much preoccupied with the practical problem around which the whole book revolves: namely, how to earn a living without losing one's soul. I weighed Thoreau's general strategy for solving this problem (which, roughly, amounts to reducing your material needs until the effort required to earn a living is no longer onerous), together with the many concrete applications of it suggested by him, testing in my imagination their applicability to my situation. This experience colored my interpretation of *Walden* considerably. I see this book as quite literally a self-help book (while admitting it is many other things as well). In particular the notion of *Walden* as provoking thought experiments that must be taken seriously is central to my understanding of the book. I would even go so far as to say that those who have not read it at a time of life when his problem is the paramount one, who do not carry out his mental experiments in deadly (or lively) earnest, or who do not at least imagine themselves in such circumstances as they read it, have missed the unique experience of reading *Walden* altogether. He tells us on the first page of the book who comprises the principal audience of the book: "Perhaps these pages are more particularly addressed to poor students. As for the rest of my readers, they will accept such portions as apply to them. I trust that none will stretch the seams in putting on the coat, for it may do good service to him whom it fits."

    At any rate, the autobiographical facts I have just recounted might help to explain one feature of the present book that some readers might find just a trifle eccentric. I will sometimes refer to my subject as Thoreau and sometimes as Henry. One of the things that make him a unique author is the extent to which readers and scholars relate to him in a personal way. If I heard a Melville scholar refer to Melville as Herman, I would suppose they were making a joke of some sort. Not so with Henry. I think of Henry as a respected older brother, one whose influence I feel strongly but must to some extent resist.

This is related to another, more important feature of this monograph. Earlier philosophical writers on Thoreau, notably Stanley Cavell and Philip Cafaro, have been eager to convince people that Thoreau should be taken seriously as a thinker and so have rather single-mindedly defended his views.[1] Partly because of their excellent work, I will assume that I will not need to work so hard just to get Thoreau a hearing. My main purpose will be to untangle what in his thinking can stand up to criticism from that which is vulnerable to weighty objections. Accordingly I will sometimes defend him and sometimes argue against him.

Finally, I think I should comment briefly on Cavell's classic book, *The Senses of Walden*. I was very privileged to be in the audience when in January 1972 Prof. Cavell came to the University of California to present his book as a series of three lectures. I had already read *Walden* by my pond in the woods and taken Thoreau very seriously indeed as a thinker and a potential guide on the path of life, but I think that hearing Cavell on Thoreau was probably one of the things that gave me the idea that I should one day write about him myself. I still think that Cavell's book is a very fine one for the sensitivity and insight with which he often discusses particular passages in Thoreau. If for that reason alone, his book is indispensable for the serious student of Thoreau. But I long ago came to realize that his broader interpretation of Thoreau is very different from mine. To some extent, this is a matter of emphasis. Cavell is very impressed with the way in which Thoreau uses literary means to display the beauty of the world to us, almost as if Thoreau holds a Wittgensteinian view that matters of value cannot be said but only shown.[2]

I agree that this is an aspect of Thoreau's writing, but, partly because I think Cavell has already explored it so effectively, I choose to emphasize another aspect of the Thoreauvian corpus: that it presents us with doctrines. It is true, and important to realize, that Thoreau is often trying to show and not to theorize. But the reason for this, in my view, is not that he holds anything like a Wittgensteinian theory that thinking about value is radically different from dealing with the truths of science and mathematics. It is rather that, like Plato and Aristotle, he belongs to what Martha Nussbaum calls "the contemplative tradition."[3] This is the tradition that holds that the *telos*, the natural goal, of love is to contemplate the love-object. Thoreau loves nature and treats it as divine: consequently, he wants to show us what it is like to contemplate the sacred aspect of things.

In addition to his insightful discussion of particular passages in Thoreau, Cavell also does sometimes attribute doctrines to him. When he does so he often seems to me to be quite wrong about what these doctrines are. In some cases, he attributes to him a position that seems to me nearly the opposite of what Thoreau actually thought. From time to time in what follows I will comment, mainly in the endnotes, on the points of similarity and those of contrast between Cavell's account and my own.[4]

Finally, I probably should say that, in what follows, it is not my purpose to prove that Thoreau was "really" a philosopher. Anyone who is familiar with his writings, especially his staggeringly immense *Journal*, knows that if he was just one thing, he was a naturalist. Nature was his single greatest subject. But he was not just one thing. What I say, simply, is that he did have philosophical ideas and theories, that he gave reasons for them, and that the ideas and the reasons are worth thinking about. This book is the result of my own attempts to deal with them.

Acknowledgments

I must thank Prof. Philip Cafaro for reading an earlier draft of this monograph and making many helpful comments on it. I have acknowledged some of them in the endnotes. I have also been helped by discussions with two other fellow Thoreauvians: independent scholar Steven Webb and Prof. Imtiaz Moosa. Among other things, their infectious enthusiasm helped maintain my faith that this project is worth doing. In addition, Brent Ranalli gave me some valuable help tracking down the source of the story about Thoreau paying his parents rent. I would also like to thank Liberty Fund for giving me the opportunity to direct two conferences on Thoreau at Concord's Colonial Inn, a building in which the Thoreau family lived for several years. These conferences were both enlightening and inspiring. Portions of "Appendix: Analogical Argument" appeared earlier in the journal *Philosophy and Literature* and are reprinted here with the kind permission of the Johns Hopkins University Press.

A Note on Citations

All quotations for Thoreau's shorter works, including "Walking," "A Plea for Captain John Brown," and "Civil Disobedience," will be from the Library of America edition of these works: Henry David Thoreau, *Collected Essays and Poems* (New York: Literary Classics of the United States, 2001). All citations for the four books that he prepared for publication will be to the companion volume, *A Week on the Concord and Merrimack Rivers, Walden; or, Life in the Woods, The Maine Woods, Cape Cod* (New York: Literary Classics of the United States, 1985). For all Thoreau's works, I will cite the sources between parentheses, in the text. Numbers in parentheses refer to page number, followed by line number or numbers (with chapter headings counting as lines), for example: (269.26). Citations to his *Journal* will be by month, day, and year of the *Journal* entry, between parentheses in the text. For all quotations from *Journal* entries dating from before the end of 1854, the edition I will be using will be the monumental Princeton edition, still in progress, of his complete works. Because entries in the *Journal* dating from 1855 to the end have not yet been published in the Princeton edition, for those I use the Houghton Mifflin edition of 1906, which is now available in a reprint: *The Journal of Henry D. Thoreau: In Fourteen Volumes Bound as Two*, ed. Bradford Torrey and Francis H. Allen (New York: Dover, 1963). Citations to all other authors will be in the endnotes. Reference to other parts of this book will be by chapter and section number, with the chapter represented by a Roman numeral and the section by an Arabic one: IV.2.

I

Context: His Life and Times

1. His Life

A word about Thoreau's life is surely in order. He is one thinker whose life is very relevant to understanding his ideas. It was a brief life, a mere 44 years and 10 months, but intensely lived.

David Henry Thoreau (he would reverse his two names while in college) was born on July 17, 1817, in Concord, Massachusetts, a town about 20 miles from Boston that already had a very proud history going back to the earliest days of colonial New England. It would be difficult to exaggerate the importance of place, and of *this* place, in his writing, his thinking, and his emotional life. Once in his *Journal* he interrupted a description of a sandy beach in a local pond with this impetuous declaration:

> —Dear to me to lie in—this sand-... And this is my home—my native soil, and I am a New Englander. Of thee O earth are my bone & sinew made—to thee O sun am I brother... To this dust my body will gladly return as to its origin. Here have I my habitat. I am of thee. (November 2, 1851)

There are many such moments in his *Journal*.

The Thoreaus of Concord were descended from Huguenots (i.e., Protestants) who fled France when persecutions resumed after the Revocation of the Edict of Nantes (1685). Henry thought they might ultimately have descended from Viking settlers of the French coast, on the theory that *Thoreau* was derived from *Thor*, the god of storm and thunder. The family always pronounced its name with the accent on the first syllable—*Thoreau*—which might have made this thought a natural one. His father, John Thoreau, was a quiet man, rather dominated by Henry's mother, Cynthia Dunbar Thoreau. She was by all accounts a woman of strong opinions, especially on moral subjects, and expressed them to all who would listen and to many who wouldn't. Henry was probably much more influenced by his mother than by his unassuming father.

John Thoreau was a shopkeeper who had a series of businesses that were not very successful until, early in the 1820s, his brother-in-law Charles Dunbar staked a claim to a deposit of quality "plumbago" (i.e., graphite) and started a business manufacturing pencils. John joined the firm and Charles, never much of a businessman (nor really much of anything else) dropped out. Soon the firm was John Thoreau and Co. At various times in the years that followed, Henry was intensely involved in the family business, doing various kinds of work. He researched graphite and pencil-lead production, found ways to make Thoreau leads smoother and less gritty, developed different degrees of lead hardness, invented a machine for drilling the pencil wood and inserting the lead without splitting the wood and gluing it together again, and introduced a substantial improvement in the machine used to grind the graphite, enabling it to produce a finer graphite dust. At one point he complained that the factory used up so much of his energy that he dreamed of its machines at night. Eventually, Thoreau Pencils became known as the finest made in America. This is in no small measure due to Henry's contributions. When he says, in *Walden*, that he had always tried to acquire strict business habits, it was literally true: he was a businessman, and a productive one, when he gave such matters his attention.

In 1833, he enrolled in Harvard, eventually earning his undergraduate degree. It was a time when education at Harvard laid considerable emphasis on the Greek and Latin classics, studied in their original languages. The aim was rote mastery of the texts, with little in the way of interpretation or analysis. In later life, he often expressed a low opinion of the education he received there—when Emerson said that they teach all the branches of knowledge at Harvard, he is supposed to have replied "all of the branches and none of the roots"—but he did acquire a lifelong love of the ancient classics, the poets more than the philosophers.

While he was at Harvard, Ralph Waldo Emerson, the most influential intellectual in America at the time, moved to Concord and the two men probably met soon after Henry graduated. It is likely that the first entry in Thoreau's *Journal*, dated October 22, 1837, refers to Emerson: "'What are you doing now?' he asked. 'Do you keep a journal?' So I make my first entry today." His *Journal* (he always referred to it in the singular) would eventually run to at least two million words. In an obvious sense, it is his major literary production. Some say it is his greatest, greater even than *Walden*.

The year he graduated from Harvard was the year of the Panic of 1837, which precipitated an economic depression. Work would be hard to find and Henry was to spend several years seeking a profession outside his home and the family pencil factory. He taught at the Center School, the local public school, but very soon resigned in a dispute over the alleged necessity of caning the students. He traveled to Maine, on ten dollars borrowed from Emerson, seeking another teaching job, but without result. He started his own school in his parent's house, then took over the Concord Academy, a private institution, where he was soon joined on the faculty by his older brother, John, Jr. But it closed after two years due to John's ill-health. At one point he made a serious effort to purchase a farm that had caught his fancy and become a farmer, but the purchase fell through. For several years, he seems to have made a heroic attempt to become a professional writer, perhaps inspired by the example of Emerson, who was one of the very first Americans to make his living largely by writing. He contributed to the *Dial*, the short-lived journal founded by Emerson and his friends, and submitted poems and essays to other publications, with some success. He lived for a while in New York, ostensibly to serve as tutor to the children of Emerson's brother William, who was a judge in Staten Island, but also to visit the offices of many editors (New York was already the publishing capital of the young country) in an effort to interest them in his writing. Except for commencing a working relationship and long-distance friendship with Horace Greeley, abolitionist and editor of the *New York Herald*, the stay in the city was more or less without result. Unless we count his years at Harvard—a period that was punctuated by many stays at home—this stay of less than one year was the longest period that he lived outside Concord. It was on another trip to New York, made to sell Thoreau pencils, that he met and befriended Walt Whitman.

    The sudden death from tetanus of his older brother in 1842, the year before the extended stay in New York, was probably a crisis in Henry's life in more ways than one. John was Henry's best friend. It was said that the brothers were "as close as twins." When John died, Henry was very ill for several days, with symptoms similar to John's, but without an apparent physical cause. He later called this strange episode "sympathetic lockjaw." But, though Henry would have been horrified to think of it this way, John's tragic and untimely end may have had a positive side. John was more extroverted than Henry, more charming and well-liked. Henry had always been in some ways in John's shadow. Now he could no longer think of himself as John Thoreau's less interesting brother. His efforts to be something on his own seem to have stepped up after this.

    In the spring of 1844, after the return from New York, there was a crisis of another sort. One day in April he went fishing with a young friend, Edward Hoar, a Harvard undergraduate. They decided to build a fire to make a chowder of the fish they had caught. For some reason they thought it would be a good idea to build the fire on top of a tree stump. The fire escaped and spread to the surrounding forest, which was dry and combustible at the time. By the time they could come back with help it was burning on a front half a mile wide. Eventually, it burned approximately 300 acres. The two might have faced criminal prosecution if it were not for the fact that young Edward's father, Samuel Hoar, a former congressman and state senator, was one of the town's most prominent citizens. He is said to have compensated at least two families who lost property in the fires. Thoreau seems to have watched the return of vegetation to the blackened landscape very intently, but with what thoughts? We get a clue from a *Journal* entry he wrote over seven years later (September 10, 1851):

> In the spring I burned over a hundred acres [*sic*] until the earth was sere and black—& by mid-summer this space was clad in a fresher and more luxuriant green than the surrounding even. Shall man then despair? Is he not a sproutland too after so many searings and witherings?

It is perhaps no coincidence that one of his last essays—the most frequently reprinted and widely read of his writings in his lifetime—was a scientific treatment of a puzzling phenomenon involving the regrowth of forests that have been clear-cut or burned (namely, the fact that the species of trees that first spring up are often completely different from those that were there before). It could be that the debacle of the fire, which I am sure was occasion of much guilt and shame (for years he would be dogged by whispers of "woods burner" behind his back), might also have spurred his life-long fascination with nature's wonderful power to rejuvenate and repair itself.[1]

It was some time in the early 1840s that he settled on a solution to the problem of how to earn his living, one that he stayed with for the rest of his life. It was memorably, if somewhat misleadingly, described by Nathaniel Hawthorne when he first met Thoreau. "For two or three years back," Hawthorne remarked in his private notebooks, "Thoreau has repudiated all regular modes of getting a living, and seems inclined to lead a sort of Indian life among civilized men—an Indian life, I mean, as respects the absence of any systematic effort for a livelihood."[2] By denying any systematic effort he must mean that Thoreau avoided a regular job, for there definitely was effort and even system of a rather chaotic sort. For over the years on a piecework basis he did jobs of many different kinds, including tutoring, carpentry, house-painting, attending to the family's graphite and pencil business, as well as digging basements and laying in their stone walls and floors. If you visit Concord today you can still see the more durable parts (some white marble posts) of a fence he built for a residence there. A job that he did rather often, because it suited him so well, was surveying. This required him to establish exact boundary lines, draw up maps, and on occasion testify in court as an expert witness. It was an ideal sort of job for someone who loved to be outdoors and did not want to report to a boss or be subject to rigidly set hours. One result is that many of his fellow Concordians thought of him as lazy, an opinion we sometimes still see today in the form of wisecracks in newspaper columns and elsewhere.

His system, if I may call it that, was to avoid a job that requires him to follow someone else's timetable. We know from his *Journal* that his days tended to follow a certain pattern: He would spend the morning doing one of his odd jobs. The afternoon would be devoted to one of his arduous walks, often of 10 miles or more, and often in the company of a friend young and strong enough to keep up with him. The evening would be spent writing up his reflections, always including an account of the day's walk, often followed by more writing and rewriting early the next morning. This is not the routine of a loafer. Really, the myth of his laziness stands the truth on its head. Consider the two million words of the *Journal*, the four books published or prepared for publication in his lifetime, including possibly the greatest book by an American, and several classic essays, all in a life of only 44 years. He was not avoiding work at all. He was doing the work that he wanted to do, and a staggering amount of it at that.

In 1845 came one of the two most famous events in his life (the other being his night in jail for nonpayment of a poll tax). For years he had been thinking of living next to one of the local "ponds" (where I live we would call them lakes). When Emerson purchased a wooded lot on the edge of Walden Pond, Henry approached him for permission to build a structure there and live in it, at least for a while. Emerson apparently liked the idea and agreed. Thoreau's need for relative freedom from distraction had become pressing because of a writing project he had in mind. He had begun to write a book, *A Week on the Concord and Merrimack Rivers*, as a sort of memorial to his departed brother (the narrative thread of the book was the last trip the two had taken together). He stayed at Walden for two years, two months, and two days. During that period, he wrote almost all of *A Week*, began to approach publishers, and in addition wrote a draft of at least 119 pages of his next book, the one that would become his masterpiece: *Walden*.[3] His stay at Walden was a period of terrific creativity and one he looked back on in later years with nostalgia.

The publication, in 1849, of *A Week* was the worst disaster of his career as a writer. After some trouble finding a publisher, he naively entered an agreement that committed him to paying for publication expenses if the book did not sell.

Whether from knavery or incompetence, the publisher did virtually nothing to promote the book. There were some reviews, but they were mixed at best. Thoreau had to take 706 copies of the 1,000 copies printed, owing the publisher $290. This was far in excess of a year of his modest income. It took him almost four years to pay the debt off, partly by stepping up his activities as a paid lecturer, but he did it, and the experience dealt the final death blow to his dream of ever being a professional writer.

Another result of this crushing disappointment was actually positive: he was in no hurry to complete and publish his next book. He worked on it for six years, scrupulously bringing it through multiple drafts. Thus *Walden* became the most polished, carefully written, thoroughly thought-out classic of the American Renaissance of the 1850s, a work of deep passion expressed in a form of crystalline perfection.[4]

While he was working on *Walden*, around 1852, his *Journal* took on a markedly different character. The earlier entries were often intended as rough, early versions of passages that were later entered into his published works. On many occasions, he tore or cut out passages or whole pages to use as drafts of his published works. After the change, the *Journal* became an end in itself. Entries became longer and more numerous, and they were focused more and more on minute observations of natural phenomena that he had made on his interminable walks. In terms of its sheer size and the amount of energy and effort that went into it, the *Journal* was obviously, and by many orders of magnitude, his major literary product. We do not know exactly why he expended this remarkable amount of effort on it, or what he intended should become of it. Did he think it would all, or much of it, be published some day? I have noticed that though he frequently discusses people he knows, he usually conceals their names, as if he means to protect their privacy. So he clearly thought others might see it someday. Beyond that, we can only guess. My guess is that it eventually became a sort of yoga, riveting his attention on nature and its ways. He once wrote (October 26, 1842), "I suppose that what in other men is religion is in me love of nature." Perhaps it was a sort of merging with the divine.

He contracted tuberculosis around the time that he was a student, and throughout his life he was troubled by periodic flare-ups of the disease that would lay him out for a while. Finally, in the spring of 1962, he began to weaken dramatically and it became plain the end was near. He spent his last weeks making final revisions in some of his writings, including "Walking" and *The Maine Woods*. I have always found the tranquility with which he departed from life a marvel and an inspiration. His sister Sophia said he told her, during those last days, that "the thought of death could not begin to trouble him," and this does seem to be true. When a friend attempted to console him, he said, "When I was a very little boy I learned that I must die and I set that down, so of course I am not disappointed now." When his Aunt Louisa told him it was time to make his peace with the Lord, he said, "I did not know we had ever quarreled, Aunt." When Sophia said to him that he was so close to "the brink of the dark river" she almost wondered what the other side looked like to him, he said, "One world at a time." In the last sentence he uttered, the only words that could be discerned were "moose" and "Indian." He was probably thinking of *The Maine Woods*, which he was still working on. Finally, as Cynthia, Sophia, and Aunt Louisa looked on, his breathing slowed and stopped at last. Sophia later said, "I feel as if something very beautiful had happened, not death."[5]

You would think that, dying at such an early age, he would have regrets over unfinished business. We do know that he had accumulated 575 pages of "Notes on Fruits and Seeds," obviously intended to be worked up into a book,[6] and that he hoped to write a book about Native Americans.[7] No doubt there were many other worthwhile things he might have done had he not been cut down. But as we will see, his theory was that the principal business of life is to live, and to live according to the promptings of one's own innermost nature. This task was already accomplished. It was done at nearly every moment of his adult life.

. . .

There is one more thing that I need to discuss before I move on from the subject of Thoreau's life: what you might call the issue of his character. Henry inspires some surprisingly (surprising to me at any rate) negative reactions in people. I have never forgotten how shocked I was when, upon first reading selections from *Walden* as an assignment in a high school English class, I came to class the next day and found that virtually all the comments the students made—and the teacher as well!—were utterly hostile. I think I was the only one who defended him.

I got the impression, I remember it very vividly to this day, that people felt that in criticizing how Americans live he was criticizing them, and that they took it personally. Some of the comments about him were really attacks on him as a person. Many of the attacks I have seen on him since, at least in the non-scholarly press, were also quite personal. Not long ago there was an essay about him, in a very prominent magazine, titled "Pond Scum," and from the title you can pretty well guess the tone of the criticisms it contained.[8]

Some personal attacks on Thoreau are simply cases of the ad hominem fallacy, the attempt to discredit an argument by discrediting the person who presents it. If it is done well, an ad hominem attack makes it hard to take the target argument seriously, at least if it comes from that particular presenter. It is as if they can talk all they want, but their microphone has been turned off. Their messages will not be received. He certainly gives some people a strong motive to launch ad hominem attacks against him. *Walden* challenges its readers in many different ways, to justify their lives and to consider very seriously if their lives are not founded upon some monstrous mistake. People do not always take kindly to being poked and jostled in this way.

But not all attacks on Thoreau as a person are ad hominem. His great subject was the greatest of them all: *How should we live?* As he attacks this question in *Walden*, he sets himself up as some sort of example. This opens him to personal attack: certain sorts of personal criticisms become logically relevant, simply because the case he argues is to some extent about himself. He says, "You people don't really have to do so-and-so, and the proof is that I don't do so-and-so." But he *did* do so-and-so! Therefore maybe you do have to do so-and-so, or at least his own case fails to prove you don't. That sort of attack is not a fallacy. It has merit, provided that it does get it right about what he is saying and gets its facts straight about what he actually did.

A possible case in point is the comment we sometimes hear that while he was at Walden he had his mother do his laundry. Actually, I hear it a lot. As Rebecca Solnit has said, there is no important writer in world literature whose laundry arrangements are so often a subject of comment. There is even a website where you can buy a Thoreau laundry bag.[9]

What might be said in response to this criticism? Thoreau's most recent biographer points out that it involves a historical mistake, as middle-class women in those days, women like Cynthia Dunbar Thoreau, did not even do their own laundry, let alone that of their adult offspring. Such housekeeping chores were done by servants, typically Irish immigrants.[10] But of course the allegation would remain that somebody other than Henry did the chore. What of that?

I suppose the proper response depends on what the objection is actually supposed to be. To me, this is by no means obvious. I strongly suspect that it is a charge of hypocrisy, that the charge is that he is haughtily setting himself up as someone who does or does not do something or other, and that this pretense is belied by his cleaning arrangements. Maybe the idea is that in *Walden* he is saying something like, "You people don't need help from anybody. Look at me! I lived at Walden as an isolated hermit and never took anyone's help!" As we will see later, in case it is not already obvious, this would be a stunningly wrong-headed misinterpretation of what he is saying.

Then again, maybe the charge is that Henry was a freeloader, a moocher who took from others and gave nothing in return. But the idea of "Thoreau the Freeloader," if that is the idea, is nearly as false as the old myth of "Thoreau the Loafer." It is true that for nearly all of his life he lived in the house of his parents, but it is also true that he paid them rent. We find meticulous records he kept of the amounts paid in his papers, sometimes on the backs of poems he was working on.[11] He also did a substantial amount of the work of building the first house that the family owned, the one they called the "Texas house." He also did many repair and maintenance jobs around the house. Every year he planted an elaborate garden, thus making a substantial contribution of food to the family. Clearly, he believed in paying your way if you can, and he made sure he could.

Again, maybe the charge is something more sophisticated, something like this: "Thoreau's economic project, of reducing his needs to a minimum so that he can spend a minimal amount of time working for pay, is only possible because he is part of an economy that is highly productive precisely because most people do not live that way, but produce goods and services full time. It assumes that most people are not living as he is." Another comment I sometimes hear that might represent the same line of reasoning is the claim that during the stay at Walden he often dined out at the Thoreau family table or those of the Emersons, the Alcotts, or the Hosmers, the idea being that the Walden project was subsidized by those who were not participating in it. I have spoken with economists who raised this objection. Whether this is a sound one depends in part on just what his project is and what sorts of claims he is making about it. These are matters that I will discuss in later chapters. For the moment I would only point out that this sophisticated version of the objection is no longer a charge of hypocrisy but rather an economic or philosophical objection to his (alleged) theory. The objection is that it is only feasible if most people don't follow it.

2. His Times

He once exclaimed in his *Journal* (December 27, 1856): "I have never got over my surprise that I should have been born into the most estimable place in all the world, and in the very nick of time, too." It is very obvious that the place of his birth suited him very well. But the times also were just right for someone who dealt with the problems that riveted his attention throughout his short life. Some of the factors and forces in contemporary or recent history that influenced him, either in posing problems or suggesting solutions, were these.

The Revolution and the Founding. When Thoreau was a young man, there were many people still living who could remember the American Revolution. The Thoreau family, and Henry's mother's family, the Dunbars, had members on both sides of that conflict. The revolution and founding of the United States as a new nation gave many writers the impression that America was a chance for humanity to start anew, avoiding the crimes and mistakes of Europe—the hereditary aristocracy, chronic war, normalized tyranny, and other horrors—and live as human beings really should live. This idea, eloquently labeled "the American Adam" by R. W. B. Leavis,[12] is very prominent in Thoreau's writings and helps explain his exhilarating sense that he can make a clean sweep of the trash and trumpery of the past and head directly toward the ideal.

Utopianism. Americans have a long tradition of building experimental communities based on their moral or political ideals. Today that tendency is somewhat in abeyance, but there was a burst of utopianism in the 1960s and early 1970s, and it was also thriving in Thoreau's day. His friend, George Ripley, founded the Brook Farm community, based on the ideas of the dignity of labor and the equitable distribution of work. Henry visited it shortly before his move to New York. Unlike Nathaniel Hawthorne, another friend, he did not find the possibility of joining the community even remotely tempting, but he certainly shared its spirit of idealism and experimentation.

The Rise of Modern Technology. Thoreau lived during the Industrial Revolution, the second most important crisis in human history, after the Agricultural Revolution of some 12,000 years ago. Indeed, he and his family were part of it, bringing a factory to previously agricultural Concord. With the Industrial Revolution came a great surge in technological development that affected every corner of life in the nations where it happened. When Henry was born, people who wished to travel over land were driven by brute muscle power, either by walking on their own legs or by being carried or hauled by animals. If they wanted to get a message to someone who was not within shouting distance, they did so by means of a written text that had to be carried to them. In his lifetime, these things changed radically, and the change was well under way when he was still young and quite impressionable. When he left for Harvard, Concord was a day's walk or a four-hour coach ride away. When he graduated and returned home, it was a train ride of less than an hour. While he was at Harvard, Samuel Morse sent the world's first telegram. While he was at Walden, Morse sent his famous message, WHAT HATH GOD WROUGHT, from Washington to Baltimore. This development aided another one: the flood of information and misinformation brought on by newspapers and other periodical publications.

Reporters could now file stories "by cable." The world was becoming a smaller, noisier, and busier place.

These developments affected Thoreau in various ways. One that might easily escape notice: He was the first of the classic American nature writers who routinely traveled to the trailhead, or even to his final destination, by rail. William Bartram, Alexander Wilson, and John James Audubon were not so fortunate. On the other hand, with one foot in each world, the before-world and the after-world, he was well situated to be struck by these developments and well motivated to pursue the issue of their meaning for human life. As we will see, his thoughts on this subject are by no means all negative or even skeptical.

Romanticism and Transcendentalism. Romanticism was a broad artistic and philosophical movement that originated in Europe beginning, in most accounts, in the writings of Jean-Jacques Rousseau (1712–1778). It was a reaction against certain aspects of the Enlightenment, especially the tendency of English empiricists and other Enlightenment thinkers to understand human life and the world by means of mechanistic models. Romantics tended to understand things in terms of organic concepts, especially the concept of growth, the way living things develop if they are in their natural environment and are not interfered with. Living things, in this way of thinking, should be thought of as developing according to their own internal natures. This fundamental tendency resulted in two further ideas: individualism (individuals should follow the promptings of their own inner selves) and a greater emphasis on emotion and one's natural drives. In terms of these ideas, Thoreau is a profoundly Romantic thinker: he was, after all, a member of a distinctly American branch of the Romantic movement: namely, Transcendentalism.

Beyond this rather simple characterization, that it was an American form of Romanticism, it is not easy to define Transcendentalism. The movement took its name from Immanuel Kant (1704–1804), who called his basic theory "transcendental idealism." Kant's transcendentalism was an attempt to resolve the philosophical problem of realism versus phenomenalism. Does the world that we seem to perceive around us exist independently of the mind—realism—or does it consist simply in our own mental perceptions—phenomenalism? Phenomenalism leads naturally to idealism, the idea that the stuff of the real world is mental and not material. Kant's compromise solution was that we can only perceive and understand the world insofar as it conforms to our modes of perception and the basic categories of our understanding. Thus the world *as it concerns* us is a product of our minds, but it is by no means a figment of our imaginations: we do perceive reality, but we can only perceive it in the human way. It is profoundly unclear what exactly American Transcendentalism has to do with the transcendentalism of Kant. The issue is clouded by the fact that the Transcendentalists had virtually no interest in abysmally profound metaphysical and epistemological problems of the sort that exercised Kant. They were primarily ethical thinkers. That is, their interest was in how we ought to live. What is the best life for human beings? This is the basic question of ethics, and it was the more or less single-minded philosophical focus of the Transcendentalists, including Emerson and Thoreau.

Emerson began his 1842 lecture, "The Transcendentalist," by defining Transcendentalism as a form of idealism: "What is popularly called Transcendentalism among us, is Idealism; Idealism as it appears in 1842. As thinkers, mankind have ever divided into two sects, Materialists and Idealists; the first class founding on experience, the second on consciousness."[13] It soon becomes clear, as one reads this essay, that his main concern is with the implications of this metaphysical utterance for practice and for the understanding of human affairs:

> In the order of thought, the materialist takes his departure from the external world, and esteems a man as one product of that. The idealist takes his departure from his consciousness, and reckons the world an appearance ... You think me the child of my circumstances: I make my circumstance. Let any thought or motive of mine be different from that they are, the difference will transform my condition and economy.[14]

Do our circumstances cause us to have the thoughts and values we have, or do our thoughts and values, and the resulting plans and intentions, transform our circumstances? As Emerson understands it, idealism implies a solution to this chicken-and-egg conundrum. Mental realities such as thoughts, values, and intentions are the primary ones, while material factors are secondary consequences. He believes that idealism implies that human life is characterized by, so to speak, a certain direction of flow: from the mental (thoughts and so forth) the physical (action). From a vast accumulation of individual actions are built the institutions that the materialist, mistakenly, thinks determine us. Thus we arrive at the bottom line:

> From this transfer of the world into the consciousness, this beholding of all things in the mind, follow easily [the Transcendentalist's] whole ethics. It is simpler to be self-dependent. The height, the deity of man is, to be self-sustained, to need no gift, no foreign force. Society is good when it does not violate me; but best when it is likest to solitude.[15]

The likeness to solitude that he has in mind here consists of the fact that the people in this society live according to the authentic promptings of their own inner natures and not according to what their fellow citizens think they ought to do or be. This is the "self-reliance" he defends in the essay of that name. The ethically ideal society would be a society of Emersonian individualists.

Thoreau's views on ethics are broadly in line with those of Emerson. For my part, I doubt that Emerson's ethics follows, logically, from metaphysical idealism in anything like the way he thinks it does. But that does not need to concern us here. As we shall see, Thoreau finds a different basis for his version of the Transcendentalist ethic. In his day, Henry was dogged by the claim that he was a mere imitator of Emerson (some wit said, "He is even working up a nose like Emerson's"). This is a view that few if any would defend today. One difference between them that will make Thoreau more attractive to some people is that he is even less concerned with metaphysics than his mentor was. His focus is even more on matters of practice, and his view of the world is also more grounded in science, in both scientific method and current scientific theories, than Emerson's was. But in ethical matters his debt to Emerson is obvious and profound.

II

Politics and the Logic of *Walden*

1. The Argument of "Civil Disobedience"

The first time Thoreau delivered "Civil Disobedience" as a lecture, the title he gave it was actually "On the Relation of the Individual to the State." That title suggested, as the present one does not, that the subject Thoreau is treating in this essay is actually much larger than a certain technique of social activism: namely, strategically violating the law. It suggests that it is about one of the great problems of political philosophy. In fact, a look at the essay itself reveals that its principal subject is actually even grander than the relation of the individual to the state and includes the very structure of the ideal polity itself.

The notion of the ideal polity is stressed by the very structure of the essay, which both begins and ends with declarations about its nature and its possibility. At the end, Thoreau envisions a process in which individuals, having attained enough moral maturity, drop out of the state altogether:

> A State which bore this kind of fruit, and suffered it to drop off as fast as it ripened, would prepare the way for a still more perfect and glorious State, which also I have imagined, but not yet anywhere seen. (224.23–6)

Those who cannot grasp, quite on their own, what this "glorious State" would be can get a quick answer simply by returning to the beginning of the essay again. It begins with the striking disclosure, "I heartily accept the motto,—'That government is best which governs least'" and proceeds almost immediately to point out its logical implications:

> Carried out, it finally amounts to this, which also I believe,—'That government is best which governs not at all;' and when men are prepared for it, that will be the kind of government which they will have. (203.2–8)

The glorious State, the best government, is a stateless society. This, of course, would be anarchy. Yet Thoreau describes it, paradoxically, as a certain sort of state or government—as, in fact, a glorious one and the best. Thoreau's essay on the technique of civil disobedience is also an essay on the ideal state and how to get there.

Before I try to shed light on any of the mysterious statements I have just made, I would like to say another word about the structure of Thoreau's essay. Because it ends where it begins, the essay suggests a literal, physical shape: namely, the circle. We have just seen one of the effects of this circular shape: for the attentive reader, it sets off the ideal state pronouncements from the rest of the text. By making the end echo the beginning, the author calls attention to both the beginning and the end.

The feeling of circularity is also suggested by the structure of the material that comes between the two ends of the essay, which consists mostly of highly abstract and abstruse observations that encircle a very concrete, central narrative section. The central section thus set off and framed (in the original edition, it was also indented) is the famous story of his incarceration for nonpayment of taxes. The structure of the essay pulls our attention in two seemingly contrary directions: toward its most abstract and ideal portions, at its two termini, and to its most concrete and realistic portions, which seem to form its nucleus. Perhaps the narrative section, like the ideal state pronouncements, can tell us something about how we are to take the essay as a whole.

Thoreau presents the narrative section as the story of a journey, as a trip into the interior of Concord's jail and into the interior of Concord itself. "It was a closer view of my native town. I was fairly inside of it." The effect of this journey into the interior of his community, paradoxically, is to make the town seem distant and alien: "It was like travelling into a far country, such as I had never expected to behold, to lie there for one night." Oddly, in yet another paradox, a paradox within a paradox, he has said that "to lie there" was like "traveling." (I will eventually have more to say about the paradoxicality of Thoreau's style.) Just as his journey alienated him from his village, it also seems to have alienated his fellow villagers from him, for he tells us that, when he emerged from the jail the next morning, they "first looked at me, and then at one another, as if I had returned from a long journey" (218.18–219.22).

This "pathos of distance," as Nietzsche would call it, is imparted to the reader as well, not merely through Thoreau's depiction of the jail—which includes curious details of the building, such as its seemingly ancient thick walls and iron gratings, and of the odd customs and habits of its inhabitants—but mainly through the drama of the event itself, which suggests to the readers the sense of the shock they might feel at being coerced by, or in the name of, their friends and neighbors. In Thoreau's case, his strange new surroundings bring with them a strange new thought: "I saw to what extent the people among whom I lived could be trusted as good neighbors and friends" (219.4–6). The simple act of forcibly locking him up in this medieval building puts his relations with them on an entirely new footing, violating the bonds of neighborliness that prevailed a moment ago.

The old bonds are repeatedly described by him, as indeed I just did, in terms of "neighborliness." I will eventually try to show that his notion of neighborliness, together with a few closely related ideas which support or build on it, are crucial for understanding the ideas in "Civil Disobedience." These ideas, I will argue, are crucial to the case he builds there for his political method and for his conception of the ideal state. They are likewise crucial to the critique he launches against the political arrangements he opposes.

Before I can try to show this, however, I will need to launch a rather elaborate discussion of another work by Thoreau: namely, *Walden*. In obvious ways, these two works are sharply different. "Civil Disobedience," much the shorter of the two, is focused rather narrowly on the problems of ethics and politics. *Walden*, on the other hand, is concerned very broadly with the problems of knowledge, of the structure of human nature, and of the nature of nature itself. Yet precisely because of this difference in subject matter, *Walden* surrounds and undergirds "Civil Disobedience," giving it context and foundations. In fact, the text of *Walden* itself encourages us to think of the connection between these two works. At the end of the chapter "The Village" there is a short passage (459.23–38) that tells, in condensed form, the story of the narrative portion of "Civil Disobedience." "Civil Disobedience," then, has the form of an expansion of a passage in *Walden* and a comment on it. You might see it as a sort of appendix to *Walden*. In what follows I will try to show that "Civil Disobedience" gains stature as a work of philosophy if it is read as such an appendix. To do so will require, as I have said, discussing *Walden* at considerable length.

2. What *Walden* Is

Walden is a very singular book. It mixes abstruse philosophical musings with very minute observations of woodchucks, pond water, ants, and other details of the natural world. It has a narrative structure of sorts, but it is a very minimal one. In this narrative, the author's own self is obsessively featured and other characters almost entirely absent. No other literary classic much resembles it. Is there a literary genre in which it *could* be placed? It may be that the most accurate answer to this question is: "None, unless it constitutes, with its subsequent imitations, a genre of its own." Nonetheless, as Stanley Cavell suggests, it can be illuminating to try to say which genre *Walden* might be seen as adopting and adapting (perhaps stretching and breaking in the process) to its own ends. Cavell recommends that we try seeing it as an instance of two, starkly different, genres: epic and prophetic writing.[1] Perhaps, as I suggested in the Preface, we might see it as a self-help manual. Again, perhaps it is a confession, a satire, or a *Bildungsroman*. It is possible, with varying degrees of ease, to see it as each one of these, or as something else altogether.

Maybe it is an instance of the literary genre that he admits is one of his own guilty pleasures as a reader: "I read one or two shallow books of travel in the intervals of my work, till that employment made me ashamed of myself, and I asked where it was then that *I* lived" (402.32–5). There are one or two obvious obstacles standing in the way of our seeing *Walden* as an example of travel writing. For one, he seems to express in this passage some sort of disapproval of this sort of writing. On the other hand, he may only be disapproving of "shallow" books of this sort. Perhaps his is not a shallow book of travel but a deep one (maybe because it is a book of deep travel).

A more serious obstacle to our seeing the book this way lies in the fact that *Walden* seems to lack a characteristic that is essential to travel books: it is a book in which the protagonist never goes anywhere. It would seem safe to assume that the idea of travel includes the notion of a person moving from one place on the map to another, typically to one at a considerable distance from the first. This assumption may not be so safe as applied to Thoreau, however, who said, "I have travelled a good deal in Concord" (326.6). Concord is, in a perfectly straightforward sense, a single place. As a matter of fact, he does speak of the sort of activity he recounts in his book as a kind of travel, though he presents it as moving in a direction different from that followed by the protagonist of the typical travel book. The movement in this book does not skim from one location to another across the surface of this world (a characteristic that would literally qualify an activity as "shallow") but downward:

> Let us settle ourselves, and work and wedge our feet downward through the mud and slush of opinion, and prejudice, and tradition, and delusion, and appearance, that alluvion which covers the globe, through Paris and London,

through New York and Boston and Concord, through Church and State, through poetry and philosophy and religion, till we come to a hard bottom and rocks in place, which we can call reality, and say, This is, and no mistake. (400.7–15)

This metaphor is one that Thoreau seems to find deeply congenial as a description of what he does. He declares, for instance, that his "head is an organ for burrowing, as some creatures use their snout and fore-paws" (400.38–9). Such metaphors suggest that one can indeed travel without going from one spot on a map to another. In fact, Thoreau does consistently speak this way, his most memorable treatment of this theme being the first two or three pages of the last chapter of *Walden*, where he tells us that stationary travel is the best sort, the kind that is truly needed: "Nay, be a Columbus to whole new continents within you, opening new channels, not of trade, but of thought" (578.6–8).

To the extent that Thoreau's book shows him in the act of using his head, his organ for burrowing, he would view it as an account of a journey. At the beginning of the book, as he is explaining why there is so much in it about himself, he tells us that he requires "of every writer ... some such account as he would send to his kindred from a distant land; for if he has lived sincerely, it must have been in a distant land to me" (325.30–3). If every writer were to comply with Thoreau's requirement, all books would be travel books, in that they would have the same function in the reader's life as that served by accounts of travel: they would give their readers an opportunity to be carried out of their present environments and into circumstances far from the ordinary and the familiar. The value they have will consist, at least in part, in whatever value one might find in vicariously encountering places distant from oneself.

The travelogue is *Walden*'s point of contact with the world of cheap literature, with reading as pure entertainment. It promises to be an opportunity to meet an amusingly eccentric hermit and other denizens of his charming forest. The promise begins with the original title page of the book, where readers would find a sketch of a curious little house with an inviting footpath that wanders from us to its doorway. This promise, and its fulfillment, surely *is* part of the book's value: it is a small but strategically placed part, like the bait on a hook at the end of a long line.[2]

Another literary genre into which *Walden* can be fit is closely related to travel writing, inasmuch as the works that belong to it typically are written *as if* they were books of travel, as accounts of imaginary journeys. This is the genre of utopian writing. Of course, Thoreau is an unusual visitor to utopia in that, aside from the fact that he goes nowhere, he does not seem to visit a utopian *state*, as visitors to utopia generally do. His utopia would seem virtually to consist of one solitary person. One of his aims, though, is identical to the primary aim that utopian authors have always pursued: to give us a convincingly detailed description of perfection. At least as important, perhaps, is the fact that he also shares what might be called the negative aim of utopian authors. It is their purpose not merely to depict the good but to give such a dense and complete representation of it that their readers feel that they now occupy a vantage outside their own society and superior to it. From this lofty position, the readers feel they can see their world from outside, and see it whole, so that they can judge its value as they never have before. Putting the book down, we return to our reality with some of the disaffection with which Lemuel Gulliver returns from the hyperrational world of the Houyhnhnms, or the male protagonists of Charlotte Perkins Gilman's feminist utopia *Herland* come back to their nonfeminist world. This sense of estrangement from the current social world seems to be precisely what the author of *Walden* wishes to achieve.

Current society is represented throughout *Walden* by the village of Concord. When Thoreau tells us the precise location of his cabin, he says it was a mile and a half south of Concord and "somewhat higher than it" (390.39–40), and that he could see the village "by standing on tiptoe" on "a hill top near by" (391.23–31). Notice also he describes the people of Concord, in the chapter called "The Village," with the same objective style he has used to depict the creatures of the forest. They appear to be simply another species of colonial mammal, like the prairie dogs with whom he seems to suggest we compare them (456.14–20). Life in the forest has evidently brought about a certain estrangement, what Marxist critics used to call the *Entfremdungseffekt*, on his perceptions of contemporary social arrangements. He wishes the reader to share this estrangement.

Of course, a book with only one developed character can be called a utopia only if one stretches the genre to the breaking point or beyond. Indeed, it may be part of Thoreau's intention to question one of the constitutive assumptions of utopian writing: that it is only in society that we can find perfect goodness. Closely analogous things can be said about forcing *Walden* into the category of travel writing, a genre based on the assumption that we acquire important knowledge when we pass from one point on the map to another. I can find one genre, though, into which it can fit much more straightforwardly than in these two cases.

In the chapter called "Conclusion," at a point in the chapter at which it would be appropriate to pause and take stock of the whole enterprise now concluding, he says this: "I learned this, at least, by my experiment; that if one advances confidently in the direction of his dreams, and endeavors to live the life which he has imagined, he will meet with a success unexpected in common hours" (580.1–4). He is speaking here to an audience for whom his experiment in living is a story they have just read, precisely as if he were pointing a moral to be drawn from this story. That is, he is presenting *Walden*, at least for the moment, as a fable.

Of course, if it is a fable, it is a very long one. It is also a rather top-heavy one, in that a far greater portion of it consists of abstract discourse than is the case in the fables of Aesop. It is also potentially very complex, as Thoreau indicates when he suggests ("this, at least") that other things might be learned from his tale. But it is not obvious that either length, complexity, or even top-heaviness should count against a narrative's being a fable.

Walden has affinities to another genre in which abstract meaning is deeply important, though the affinities are in this case more counterintuitive and less exact than the last. To guess which genre I have in mind, one need only consider some of the most salient features of the tale that Thoreau tells. He tells it, speaking in the first person, about himself alone. Fundamentally, it is the story of the author's apparently successful attempts to change, not the world, but his view of the world. It is not the things in his environment that he seeks to manipulate but the things that are in his mind. In particular, it has come to worry him that some of these things do not belong in his mind at all and that they are so intertwined with the things that do belong there that it is hard to distinguish those that belong from those that do not. The method by which he solves the problem thus presented is to proceed (while still in solitude) to empty his mind of these things and put them back only as dictated by necessity. He does this explicitly in the first chapter and, in less obvious ways, throughout the book. Once the method has been followed, he will be able to carry out his normal activities on a solid foundation.

It will be obvious to any student of the history of philosophy that what I have just described is a *Cartesian meditation*. Yet, just as we can only view this book as a book of travel by violating the requirement that it describe movement from one place to another, so we can only regard it as a Cartesian meditation by doing violence to what alert students know about Rene Descartes's own *Meditations*. One deep difference between Thoreau's book and that of Descartes lies in the simple fact that the mental contents that Descartes was rearranging were beliefs about how the world is, while in Thoreau's case the contents are different. Thoreau is concerned about commitments, attachments, and, above all, *practices*: things that he does. Accordingly, the method he uses does not consist merely in thinking, as Descartes's method does, but in doing as well. He goes to the woods, he tells us, to try an experiment. He is trying out certain ideas and expects to learn something from what actually happens. He also expects us to learn something from his narration of these events.

Another difference between Thoreau's meditation and that of Descartes is the sharply opposed treatment of the idea of dreaming in the two works. In Descartes's narrative, the author's motive for developing and carrying out his distinctive method is to forestall a horrifying possibility that is symbolized, for him, by the thought that, for all he knows for certain, the experiences he is having might all be a dream. It is to exclude this possibility—the possibility that he might be trapped, alone, inside his mind—that he builds the rigid structure of proofs that comprise most of his book.

If the attitude toward dreaming reflected in Descartes's book is one of aversion, then that in Thoreau's is one of attraction: he advises you, in the stated moral of his story, to go "in the direction of" your dreams. Nor, as everyone knows, does he find the aloneness represented by dreaming to be such a terrible thing. He invites us at one point to pity the inmates of crowded cities with the comment: "Consider the girls in a factory,—never alone, hardly in their dreams" (430.38-9). Surely, the different ways in which Descartes and Thoreau treat dreaming suggests that there is some deeper difference between them that underlies this one. As we will see in II.4 and II.5, this is indeed the case, and we will also see that the deeper difference is closely related to the contrast between the Thoreauvian focus on action and the Cartesian focus on thought. It is also related to another contrast, which I will also explore in II.4: the sharp difference between two views of the significance and value of necessity.

Then we will be able to see why *Walden* follows as well as denies and violates the requirements of the Cartesian meditation. We will also see something about how these functions are connected with its working as a stationary travelogue and a deviant utopia. In the Appendix, I will also discuss it as a gigantic, top-heavy fable.

3. Proof and Necessity

There is one feature of *Walden* that seems more antithetical to the *Meditations* of Descartes, and indeed of any work of philosophy, than any other. The hard skeletal structure of Descartes's book is an articulated assemblage of proofs allegedly leading the reader from wavering doubt to firm certainty. Thoreau's book, on the other hand, will appear to most philosophers to be utterly boneless: in particular, it seems to contain nothing such a person could easily recognize as a proof. Its author seems deeply uninterested in proving anything, perhaps hostile to the very idea of proof.

His favorite rhetorical device is one that seems at the farthest possible remove from proof: namely, paradox. Whereas proof aims at compelling the reader to agree, and at depicting the author's idea as if it *has to be* true, a paradox represents the idea as if it *could not be* true, thus appearing to make agreement impossible. It represents the idea as if it were contradictory, as if it contradicted either itself or well-known facts. "The swiftest traveller is he that goes afoot" (364.22). This seems to contradict the well-known fact that trains travel many miles per hour faster than pedestrians do. "Only the defeated and deserters go to the wars, cowards that run away and enlist" (579.2–3). This seems close to being *self*-contradictory. After all, bravery in battle is a sort of paradigm that, for most of us, specifies what "courage" means. Thoreau's statement seems to say that those who are most clearly courageous are all cowards. In *Walden* there is an abundance of statements that seem designed to baffle you in one or the other of these two ways: "For the most part, we are not where we are, but in a false position" (583.5–6); "I have always been regretting that I was not as wise as the day I was born" (400.33–4); "It is a ridiculous demand which England and America make, that you shall speak so that they can understand you" (580.15–16); "I cannot exaggerate enough even to lay the foundation of a true expression" (580.33–4). The list of examples could easily grow very long indeed.

Odd as it is, the paradoxical style is an ancient one, and we have no trouble finding classic writers who tended to express themselves in paradoxes: Lao Tzu, for instance, and Chuang Tzu, Jonathan Swift, Oscar Wilde, and Nietzsche. All these authors were masters of the brilliant and stunning paradox. On the other hand, it might be useful to think of examples of authors who were anti-paradoxical. These might include, for instance, Confucius, Aesop, Montaigne, Dr. Johnson, Benjamin Franklin, and G. E. Moore. The latter sort of writers are pursuing a strategy that contrasts sharply with that of the paradoxicalists. Take, for instance, Dr. Johnson's riposte to Jean Jacques Rousseau's idea that all distinctions of social status are artificial and ought to be ignored: "A man with a good coat upon his back meets with a better reception than he who has a bad one."[3] In saying this, Johnson is not trying to stun you with the seemingly impossible; rather, he is presenting you with the evidently inescapable. He is trying to build a case on the basis of the clearly true. The opposite of the paradox is the truism, and the truth is after all what the anti-paradoxical author is trying to get you to believe. This is of course obvious. It is not so obvious what the paradoxicalists are after. Are they rejecting truth altogether? Are they pointing toward a truth that is beyond words? I will soon try to show that there is a third possibility, but for the moment I will simply point out something that the paradoxicalists are apparently *not* trying to do: it seems that they are not trying to build a case that, given that you accept one idea as true, you must also believe some other idea, one that you do not yet believe but soon will. This of course is just what people who prove things are doing.

And yet, near the beginning of *Walden*, in a place where we might expect him to present the fundamentals of his philosophical method and tell us the constraints within which it will operate, he states flatly, "No way of thinking or doing, however ancient, can be trusted without proof" (329.22-4). This is a surprising statement, and strikingly categorical. A philosopher is apt to suppose that Thoreau is speaking frivolously or carelessly here, given that there is so much in the book that seems to run counter to the very idea of proof. Actually, I think he is speaking circumspectly and very much in earnest. To see how this can be, however, we need to look more closely at the idea of proof. One of the most influential presentations of the notion of proof is the one given to us by Descartes. In his version, which still has a firm grip on many minds, this idea really has two parts. A proof starts with premises that are known for certain to be true. In the case of the most fundamental premises, upon which all further reasoning rests, they are ones that *cannot* be false. A proof also includes a structure that is such that the truth-value of the premises is transferred, without loss, to the conclusion that rests on them. Granted that it is the case that Socrates is a man, and that all men are mortal, it would have to be the case that Socrates is mortal.

What all this comes to is that, as I have said, proof in this sense depicts the author's idea (the conclusion) as something that in some way "has to be" true: it exhibits *necessity*. Moreover, it does not merely represent necessity but actively carries it out, imposing it on the reader. It traps the reader into agreeing with the author, with no realistic hope of escape. Not only does it *have to be* true, the reader *has to* believe it.

Thoreau has quite a bit to say in *Walden* that is relevant to estimating the value of proof understood in this way, as something that necessitates agreement. Necessity is a subject that he treats quite deliberately throughout the book, and there is one thing that becomes very clear in his treatment of it: he regards it in some general way as a bad thing. The reason for this attitude lies in the impact that necessity has on human life. Consider the following passage, one of many that could be cited to make the same point:

> But men labor under a mistake. The better part of the man is soon ploughed into the soil for compost. By a seeming fate, commonly called necessity, they are employed, as it says in an old book, laying up treasures which moth and rust will corrupt and thieves break through and steal. (327.6–9)

He is describing two mistakes here, under which he is saying that men labor: one is the placing of material goods above ones that are more important; the other is a deeper error, which makes the first one possible. It consists in seeing necessity where there is none. The farmer's idea that he has to spend almost every available moment caring for land, machinery, crops, and livestock completely forecloses the question of whether it is good or desirable that he do so. If he really has to do it, the question of whether he should is moot and a waste of time.

Actually, the fact that necessity is a major theme in *Walden* is obvious. Much of "Economy," the first and longest chapter, is an attempt to resist the constraining power that "necessaries of life" have over human beings. These things, the actual necessities themselves, are really less numerous, he claims, than we thought, and the necessity that characterizes them is often less binding than it at first appears. This point, though, important as it is, only deals with one sort of necessity, and there are others that also figure prominently in *Walden*. The sort of necessity that we are dealing with here, the sort that characterizes the "necessaries of life," might be called vital necessity. Here necessity is something that characterizes a particular class of things, the things we have to have if we are to live. This is not the same thing as *logical* necessity, which characterizes the relationship that holds between premise and conclusion. This is the sort of necessity that exists in the event that that, if a set of premises happens to be true, then the conclusion that is based on them would have to be true. This sort of necessity was obviously prominent in my description, above, of the Cartesian notion of proof.

We need to look at Thoreau's view of each of these two sorts of necessity separately. They are, after all, quite different things. I will deal with his views on vital necessity below, in II.4 and II.5. For the moment, I will focus his view of logical necessity.

One might think that he is capable of tolerating the rigid connection between premise and conclusion, should he wish to do so, while resisting the coercive power of our notions about the things necessary for life. After all, he could claim—couldn't he?—that ironclad logic shows that we *have to* agree with his conclusion that there are very few things that we absolutely need and that they are easily maintained. You must agree with me—resistance is futile!

This is not the position he chooses to take. The position he does take is in a way more radical than this. He does not merely resist necessity in the contents of his thoughts, he also resists necessity in the very structure of thought itself: that is, he not only resists, as much as he can, attributing necessity to some object or other (such as food, clothing, or shelter), he also puts effort into avoiding the state of mind in which one accepts a certain thought because the evidence dictates that one must accept it.[4]

To a philosopher in the Cartesian tradition (and in this respect many contemporary, English-speaking philosophers are in the Cartesian tradition) the resistance to logical necessity will sound absurd. After all, the sort of necessity Thoreau is resisting here seems to be an indispensable condition of the highest good that the intellect can produce: namely, knowledge. Without the bond of necessity that ties the parts of a proof together, its premises do not transform the conclusion into something that we know, even if we do know the premises themselves. Further, and more seriously, what is the alternative to thinking the necessary thought? It seems that the only other option open to us is to think whatever we jolly well feel like thinking, that the alternative to submitting to logical necessity is that of following one's whims.

Part of his reply to the first of these two objections, the one that accuses him of rejecting the very foundations of knowledge, would be to claim that knowledge, as defined by those who would raise this objection, is not as good a thing as they think it is. Its effects on human life are often more evil than good. He defends this rather startling idea in "Economy":

> Most men, even in this comparatively free country, through mere ignorance and mistake, are so occupied with the factitious cares and superfluously coarse labors of life that its finer fruits cannot be plucked by them. Their fingers, from excessive toil, are too clumsy and tremble too much for that. Actually, the laboring man has not leisure for a true integrity day by day; he cannot afford to sustain the manliest relations to men; his labor would be depreciated in the market. He has no time to be anything but a machine. How can he remember well his ignorance—which his growth requires—who has so often to use his knowledge? (327.22–32)

Clearly, he is saying that the reason "the laboring man" in this country cannot live as well as he might lies in the nature of his work, which incapacitates him for the best sort of life. Why does it incapacitate him? In themselves, Thoreau's metaphors about how work-coarsened hands cannot pluck life's finest fruits are not very helpful in answering this question. What we want to know is just what characteristics of the worker's life are represented by the trembling clumsiness of those hands, and how it is that the laborer's work causes it. Almost at once, however, he throws out a comment that sheds a bright ray of light on these metaphors and on much else that he is doing in *Walden*: the problem with the laborer's work is that it requires him so often to use his knowledge, thus preventing him from remembering his ignorance—"which his growth requires."

It is not very surprising that the characteristic of the workers that prevents them from living as well as they might—an inability to "remember" their ignorance—is a defect in their awareness. There is an ancient tradition in the wisdom literature of both the East and the West that warns us that what will eventually destroy us is not an external enemy but a deficiency in our own minds. What *is* rather surprising is that the feature of their work that causes this deficiency is not its mindlessness but virtually the opposite: the fact that it relies so much on the very good that the Cartesian philosopher seeks—knowledge. We must notice, however, that the valuable alternative to knowledge is not ignorance, at least not as such. Thoreau has also said, in the same passage, that people who lose themselves in "superfluously coarse labors" usually do so "through mere ignorance and mistake." Ignorance causes bad things to happen, at least sometimes. There seems to be a difference, however, between *acting in* ignorance on the one hand and *remembering* one's ignorance on the other. Acting through ignorance is bad, but remembering one's ignorance for the sake of one's growth is good. And this good use of ignorance tends to be crowded out of consciousness by excessive reliance on one's knowledge. Excessive reliance on knowledge tends to cause the bad use of our ignorance to take over our lives.

So far, what Thoreau is saying here is still rather obscure, but one thing is perfectly clear. He is saying that acting in ignorance is not the only alternative to relying on knowledge. Perhaps he would also deny that thinking what we jolly well please is the only alternative to thinking the thought that necessity dictates. That he would indeed deny this is suggested by a comment he makes about the other sort of necessity he seeks to diminish and resist: namely vital necessity. Turning to the problem of the individual who has managed to meet these necessities (properly understood), he asks, "What does he want next? ... When he has obtained those things which are necessary to life, there is another alternative than to obtain the superfluities; and that is, to adventure on life now, his vacation from humbler toil having commenced" (334.39–335.6).

Seeking superfluities is not the only alternative to the seeking of necessities of life. There is also something he calls "adventuring on life." Similarly, we might wish to say that acting out of ignorance is not the only alternative to using one's knowledge. There is also the possibility of remembering ignorance in a way that makes growth possible. This analogy seems to be a close one—seems, in fact, to be more than an analogy, since the description of the third alternative sounds in each case like more or less the same thing. "Growth," meaning the sort of personal transformation he has in mind here, is just the sort of thing that could be thought of as an "adventure." As we will see in a moment, this analogy can be carried through into the realm of logic, with the notion of the adventure of growth opening up a third option, an alternative to both the thought that is necessary and the thought that is merely groundless.

4. Proof and Possibility

Henry tells us, rather mysteriously,

> We might try our lives by a thousand simple tests; as, for instance, that the same sun which ripens my beans illumines at once a system of earths like ours. If I had remembered this it would have prevented some mistakes. This was not the light in which I hoed them. (330.37–331.1)

What sort of truth could possibly be established by such "tests"? Perhaps a better question to ask, because somewhat more concrete, is, What sorts of "mistakes" might they prevent?

We receive a clue as to what sorts of mistakes these are in the even more Delphic comment that immediately follows: "The stars are the apexes of what wonderful triangles! What distant and different beings in the various mansions of the universe are contemplating the same one at the same moment!" (331.1–2). The triangles, it would seem, consist of the lines of vision that connect different beings (ones that are literally alien to one another) with the same star, together with the lines of thought connecting these beings with each other, as one of them contemplates the existence of the other. The contemplation of other "mansions of the universe," in addition to our own planet, reveals to us the possibility of radically different ways of seeing. It is easy to imagine a broad range of mistakes that such a test might prevent, and what these mistakes have in common is that they take for granted that there is only one way of seeing. "This is the only way, we say; but there are as many ways as there can be drawn radii from one centre"

(331.32–3). What is revealed by such "tests" as this is not necessity at all but its very opposite: possibility.

Here is an example of a test that does just that. Thoreau describes in the section of "Economy" on our need for clothing, in which he is attempting to minimize the extent of the necessity to which this presumed "necessary of life" subjects us: "I sometimes try my acquaintances by such tests as this—Who could wear a patch, or two extra seams only, over the knee? Most behave as if they believed that their prospects for life would be ruined if they should do it" (340.9–13). The test he is describing here runs through three phases: First, he describes a course of action in a manner that presents it as a distinct possibility, as something that can be done. Next comes his hearer's immediate reaction, which is that this course of action is not possible at all, that they cannot do this. The presumable third phase, which in this case we can only imagine, is the audience's struggle to display this ironclad necessity, at least to its own satisfaction. Thoreau does not expect this attempt to be very successful. If the notion that one's "prospects for life would be ruined" without expensive, fashionably attractive clothing were indeed true, that *would* mean that such things are necessary (this, in fact, can serve as a definition of what vital necessity is), but he thinks that the falsity of this notion is obvious.

There are many moments in *Walden* where we need not imagine this struggle to display necessity, because it takes place in our own minds. Often, as in the following passage from the section on our need for shelter, the startling possibility is described in sufficiently convincing detail that it constitutes to some extent a challenge thrown, not to the author's acquaintances, but to the reader:

> Formerly, when how to get my living honestly, with freedom left for my proper pursuits, was a question which vexed me even more than it does now, ... I used to see a large box by the railroad, six feet long by three wide, in which the laborers locked up their tools at night; and it suggested to me that every man who was hard pushed might get such a one for a dollar, and, having bored a few auger holes in it, to admit the air at least, get into it when it rained and at night, and hook down the lid, and so have freedom in his love, and in his soul be free. This did not appear the worst, nor by any means a despicable alternative. (345.26–37)

Faced with this suggestion, a reader, at least one that reads as Thoreau wants to be read, will search for some reason why this actually is a "despicable alternative," despite what he says. Would I be able to read in bed at night? Would such an arrangement afford enough protection against thieves? Would the rain come in through the augur holes meant to let in air?

Of course, Thoreau does not think you will be moved by these thoughts to actually take up residence in a tool box. (Note the ominous ambiguity in his phrase "to admit the air *at least*"). But the tendency such thoughts have, along with others that arise in response to similar challenges from Thoreau, is to shrink the extent of the necessities imposed on us by our need for such things as shelter. At moments like this—and there are many of them in *Walden*—the book is like a Cartesian meditation in which the roles of reader and author have been reversed. Ordinarily, Descartes, and most philosophers, are in the position of someone who sees that certain things must be so, and are confronted with readers who do not see it (at least, not yet). Accordingly, they display this necessity to their readers, one step at a time. Here, on the other hand, the author is confronted with readers who see necessities that are invisible to the author, who see necessities that he regards as illusions. He challenges them to display this necessity to themselves, to construct it one step at a time. This effort represents an uphill climb, more or less steep. A reader who tries it in earnest, giving *Walden* the sort of close and personally involved attention its author wishes, will not be able to press the outer limits of necessity as far as they had extended before this effort began. The effect of reading the book is to pull those limits in, to shrink the realm of necessity.

This effect explains much of the logic of *Walden*. Truly, the entire book is just such a "test" as this. Precisely as he challenges us with countless smaller questions, so also he asks, in effect, why we don't live in the woods and work in a beanfield as he did. He does not—contrary to a popular misreading of *Walden*—expect us to go and live in the woods, no more (or at least not much more) than he expects us to live in toolboxes. Later (II.5) we will see why this is true and how important it is to the way Thoreau's logic works. For the time being, the point is that the tests he invites us to try tend to shrink the realm of necessity and so to expand that of pure possibility, to include possibilities that we had never even hoped for.

I submit that Thoreau's mysteriously categorical pronouncement, that no "way of thinking or doing ... can be trusted without proof" begins to make sense and to cohere with the rest of *Walden*, even begins to explain the entire book, if we suppose that a large part of the "proof" he proposes consists of trying such tests as these. Certainly a classical scholar like Thoreau would be vividly aware that "proof" comes ultimately from *probare*, which means to test, and especially to find the value of something. A whiff of the same idea survives in such expressions in ordinary English as *printer's proofs*, a photographer's *proof sheets* (indicating how well or poorly the negatives have turned out), and the *proving grounds* on which dangerous new vehicles are tested for speed, safety, and other valuable characteristics. For Thoreau, the activity of soundly evaluating (determining the value of) proposed ways of thinking and doing must include ruthlessly testing their claims to be the thing we have to do.

If he is almost disdainful of proof in one familiar sense of the word, the same cannot be said of this other sort of proof. Such tests, however, require him to do the very opposite of what "proofs" usually aim to accomplish. Instead of forging new bonds of necessity, belief-traps to hold his readers in place, he breaks up old bonds, setting you free.

Now we can see how appropriate one of his favorite literary methods is: namely, his use of paradox. As I have already pointed out, a claim strikes one as paradoxical because it appears to clash with facts that one feels entitled simply to take for granted or because of a felt clash with something even more fundamental: one's sense of the requirements of reason itself. The dominant feeling of a reader encountering a deliberate paradox is a feeling of being subjected to a sort of mental violence. With a sharp concussion, one's own world has collided with that of the author, in a way that makes the world of the author feel alien to one's own. Obviously, this is not the sort of feeling that I would want to cause in you if I were trying to force you into my world. On the other hand, it can help me to make a certain sort of point very persuasively: it can vividly indicate that someone can violate seemingly fundamental laws of thought. It becomes both more obvious and more difficult to forget that someone thinks very differently from the way you now think. It shows that you *could* think in this alien way as well. By realizing this, I push back necessity and extend the freedom of pure possibility.[5]

This way of understanding what *Walden* is about contrasts sharply with a suggestion made by Stanley Cavell that I have already mentioned. This is the notion that we should read it as an instance of prophetic writing. This suggestion is based on Cavell's notion that the book is very repetitive and sometimes boring. Prophets, Cavell tells us, believe they have a moral license to inflict suffering on their audiences, including the pain of boredom. The idea, I take it, is that a prophet is trying to put you on the morally straight path, and this justifies inflicting coercive penalties on you if you fail to fall in line. Cavell thinks that *Walden* shares another feature of the words of the Hebrew prophets: namely, "the periodic confusions of their authors' identities with God's."[6] This would seem to mean that Thoreau sees some of his words as actually being the words of God and not of an individual human being at all, that they have a degree and kind of authority that cannot belong to a finite individual. All this is of course deeply mistaken if the interpretation I am taking here is true. In the great monotheistic religions, the ideas of God, in relation to a mere human being, represent a truly unlimited sort of authority: to dissent from them, once they are understood, is unthinkable. Imposing this sort of authority on one's readers is the opposite of what, in my view, Thoreau seeks to do. It would be to place one more chain on them, to push them deeper into slavery.

5. Thoreau's Vitalism

This still leaves unanswered the problem with which I ended II.3: Once we have avoided the necessity imposed on us by those wiser than ourselves, we seem to be left only with undifferentiated possibility. Insofar as Thoreau avoids what philosophers have traditionally called "proof," he seems to have abandoned the most obvious sort of grounding that human action can have. Whatever we do next, is it not simply *groundless*? What guide for action is left, other than mere whim? To put it another way, what *positive* standard of value, if any, does Thoreau have to offer?

The answer to this question lies in the fact that the meaning "proof" has for Thoreau is not exhausted by the bare notion of revealing possibility. There is an additional element involved. It is an idea that, like the notion of discovering new possibilities, permeates *Walden*. Unlike that notion, though, it is distinctly normative and ethical in nature: it presents a positive guide for action.

He expresses this idea by many different means, but he presents it most directly in the chapter he called "Higher Laws":

> Every man is the builder of a temple, called his body, to the god he worships, after a style purely his own, nor can he get off by hammering marble instead. We are all sculptors and painters, and our material is our own flesh and bones. Any nobleness begins at once to refine a man's features, and meanness or sensuality to imbrute them. (499.16–21)

The analogy Thoreau suggests here, between the body and a building, takes on some extra weight when read in the context of the rest of *Walden*: the book contains definite notions about buildings and architecture. As he says in another passage, much earlier in the book,

> What of architectural beauty I now see, I know has gradually grown from within outward, out of the necessities and character of the indweller, who is the only builder,—out of some unconscious truthfulness, and nobleness, without ever a thought for the appearance; and whatever additional beauty of this kind is

destined to be produced will be preceded by a like unconscious beauty of life. (360.2–8)

Just as the real architect of a house—the author of its distinctive character—is its "indweller," so the real architect of the body is *its* indweller. When Thoreau is speaking of the individual directly (and not emblematically, through the medium of discussions of other subjects, such as architecture) he usually calls this indweller one's "genius." "Genius" is one of his most characteristic words. He speaks of one's genius, most typically, as in some way prompting or guiding conduct.[7] He would admit that there is much about a particular individual that is not there because of the individual's own genius. In fact, the architectural analogy implies as much. The indweller is not the person who places one brick of the house upon another. Similarly, the individual does not assemble the cells of his or her own body. The flesh of your face, for instance, is a product of many factors distinct from your self. However, anything about it that makes it a living human face—its habitual expression, for instance—is due to your body's indweller and discloses it to us. Your face has this fundamental ambiguity, that it is at once a physical mechanism and a living, human physiognomy.

For Thoreau, human life itself has two aspects: an inner aspect and an outer one. In the two passages just quoted, these aspects stand in a certain definite relation to one another: in them, life is presented as a process in which the current of cause and effect flows from the inside to the outside. It is, so to speak, centrifugal. Obviously, it is also possible for causation to flow in the other direction. It is open to me, for instance, to act on the basis of the ideas of other people regarding what I should do, ideas which are not mine. This is not an uncommon occurrence. But Thoreau would say that, to the extent that this is the way causation flows in my conduct, I am not (so far) a living person.

From this idea an important conclusion appears to follow, at least if we make two assumptions that appear plausible on their face and which, at any rate, Thoreau clearly does make. First, from the fact that he exhorts us not to conduct ourselves in this way, it is clear that he thinks we are capable of doing so by choice. Second, and for the same reason, it is also clear that he assumes the life we would thereby sacrifice is a precious thing and a tragic loss. It would seem to follow that, by making such a choice, one suffers a loss, falling from the position of a living human being to that of a mere mechanism. Such would be the only possible result of switching control of one's conduct from one's own genius to the various powers that dominate one's environment. This, of course, is the ethical idea that Emerson thought follows logically from metaphysical idealism. In *Walden*, though, it is stripped of its metaphysical garb and presented as a psychological or anthropological observation. The claim is based on an understanding of the nature of human life.

Together, these three ideas—the conception of life as centrifugal, the assumption that life is good, and the notion that it is possible to function in a contrary way by choice—elevate the notion of life to the position of a standard of value by which choices can be evaluated. It enables us to distinguish some courses of action as good and others as not good. It seems appropriate to call this standard Thoreau's vitalism.[8] It requires him to say that the promptings of one's genius have considerable authority as a guide to conduct. This is precisely the conclusion he does draw, in a particularly robust form: "No man ever followed his genius till it misled him. Though the result were bodily weakness, yet perhaps no one can say that the consequences were to be regretted, for these were a life in conformity to higher principles" (495.8–12).

This strong conclusion regarding the authority of individual genius helps to explain his warning against trusting ways of thinking and doing, however ancient they might be, without proof. To trust without proof is to follow a standard other than one's own genius. Clearly, arguments that merely reveal possibilities cannot, by themselves, serve to provide a grounding for human action, but matters are quite different if we place them in the context of a larger process in which individuals discover the bent of their own geniuses and follow them. This larger process, I submit, is the "proof" without which ways of thinking and doing cannot be trusted. The activity of revealing possibility is far from comprising the whole of this process. But it can make an indispensable contribution to it. Genuine proof, the actual test of what our genius demands of us, is to be found in the conduct of the person to whom the proof applies. It consists of the trials we carry out in our own lives. Words that push back the limits of necessity, including the words of *Walden*, can serve to suggest new paths to be explored and to demolish obstructions that might otherwise prevent any exploration at all.

As far as genuine proof is concerned, the sort of writing we find in Thoreau's book is both indispensably necessary and, at the same time, radically insufficient. This can account for the ambivalence he expresses, otherwise rather curious, to the activity of reading. He praises it in lofty terms in the chapter on "Reading," and yet his comments about it in the first two paragraphs of the very next chapter, "Sounds," are almost derogatory. On the one hand, he says things like this: "The student may read Homer or Aeschylus in the Greek without danger of dissipation or luxuriousness, for it implies that he in some measure emulate their heroes, and consecrate morning hours to their pages" (402.35–7). On the other hand, he says, "What is a course of history or philosophy, or poetry, no matter how well selected, or the best society, or the most admirable routine of life, compared with the discipline of looking always at what is to be seen? Will you be a reader, a student merely, or a seer?" (411.10–14). In the latter passage, he seems anxious to assert the all-importance of direct experience. The sentence that immediately precedes it in the text bears a striking similarity in both tone and syntax to the caveat about trusting without proof, but with a rather different meaning: "No method nor discipline can supersede the necessity of being forever on the alert" (411.8–10). If any way of thinking or doing is to be trusted, it must first withstand a critical process based a detailed awareness of concrete reality.

Thoreau believes that one individual's genius is apt to differ from that of another and may, in any given case, may be "a very crooked one" (366.37), as his is. For this reason, his vitalism necessarily leads to a conception of the good life which is *deeply* pluralistic. This is an implication that his readers often miss. It may be obvious that the idea of "genius" is a fundamental norm for Thoreau, but it is much less obvious that he is a pluralist about the good life. His pluralism is slightly obscured by the narrative aspect of *Walden* itself, which is an account of his own individual project and yet, at the same time, a picture of the human good itself, as if his own peculiar way of life is simply the one and only good life.

However, he declares quite explicitly that the good life is by nature profoundly plural:

> I would not have any one adopt my mode of living on any account; for, beside that before he has fairly learned it I may have found out another for myself, I desire that there may be as many different persons in the world as possible; but I would have each one be very careful to find out and pursue his own way, and not his father's or his mother's or his neighbor's instead. (378.33–9)

Despite this explicit disclaimer, Henry is frequently viewed, in effect, as the dogmatic preacher of an ethic of living off the land. Perhaps some of his readers think that he only has such pluralistic sentiments when he is thinking about the matter in abstract terms, although, as soon as he turns to applying his conception of the good life to the problems of human existence, he expects others to do as he does. Yet even in the latter sort of context he repeats the disclaimer, suitably adapted to the concrete matter at hand.

A case in point is to be found in the highly provocative discussion of philanthropy which stands as a sort of grand finale for the "Economy" chapter.

I think it will be worthwhile to take a close look at the philanthropy discussion, partly because it illustrates the point that I have just made, but also because it is very interesting in and of itself. In addition, it brings into the foreground another aspect of Thoreau's ethics, in addition to its deep pluralism, that has so far only lurked in the background of my comments here.

6. Philanthropy versus Virtue

Thoreau launches his rather shocking attack—yes, attack!—on philanthropy for a very specific reason. He wants to answer a certain criticism of his project of living at Walden Pond, one to which he has already referred on the first page of the book (325.17–18). The criticism goes like this. Fundamentally, his project is an attempt to reduce, to the bare minimum possible, the amount of time he spends producing the necessities of life, so that he produces only what he really does need. The purpose of this effort is to be able to spend more time on the activities that serve best to realize his own individual genius, activities like writing and contemplation, which he finds in his case—given the disaster of *A Week*—have little or no market value. However, by producing no more than what *he* needs, he also minimizes his production of what *others* need. The objection is that this leaves little or nothing for philanthropic purposes. "All this is very selfish, I have heard some of my townsmen say" (379.34–5). This presents him with a serious ethical problem. If philanthropy is ethically paramount, then surely he has a moral obligation to leave his little house by the pond, give up his dream of being a thinker and a writer, participate fully in the economy, and toil for the good of his fellow human beings. Why not?

His response to this problem is first of all to grasp the nettle, admitting that he is not engaged in "philanthropy," at least not in the sense contemplated in this objection. At the same time he will deny the underlying ethical assumption on which the criticism is based. This assumption is the idea that philanthropy, or deliberate altruism "with kindness aforethought" (380.33), is a very important virtue, perhaps the highest. Against it he fires a fusillade of arguments. I can identify eight (or more, depending on how we interpret them) that seem particularly important. In the following pages, I will give my account of what they are, freely drawing connections or supplying missing steps. My aim will be to imaginatively reconstruct the line of reasoning reflected in his words, using various hints and suggestions that his words supply. Such a sympathetic reading, I will maintain, shows them to be surprisingly cogent.

First, he tells us of a sort of experiment that he has tried, very different from the master-experiment of his stay at Walden:

> There are those who have used all their arts to persuade me to undertake the support of some poor family in the town; and if I had nothing to do—for the devil finds employment for the idle—I might try my hand at some such pastime as that. However, when I have thought to indulge myself in this respect, and lay their Heaven under an obligation by maintaining certain poor persons in all respects as comfortably as I maintain myself, and have even ventured so far as to make them the offer, they have one and all unhesitatingly preferred to remain poor. (380.3–8)

I think the force of this comment comes from the fact that the reader immediately understands why these people "unhesitatingly" preferred to remain poor. If we try to imagine the sort of routine he was proposing to these people—that every two weeks, say, he would directly hand over to the head of the family some coins earned in one of his many enterprises (carpentry, perhaps, or surveying, "for I have as many trades as fingers," 369.5–6), so that they could then spend them on themselves—it becomes painfully obvious that this would be a degrading position for them to be in. It is surely their decent pride in their own human dignity that prompts them to prefer being cold and hungry to receiving "help" like this.

Against this, a defender of philanthropy might reply, "Of course this would be degrading. That is because the relationship that this sort of philanthropy would establish between Henry and the poor family would be so personal. The family would be getting the money directly from someone they know. That is why philanthropic relationships are best done through relatively impersonal charitable organizations or, better yet, the even more impersonal and machine-like organization of the modern welfare state. This might well not be degrading at all." I think Thoreau might reply to this along the same lines as some of his comments on vegetarianism in "Higher Laws." There, he gives an explanation for his abstention from animal food that seems relevant to the issue here. The explanation he gives is admittedly rather mysterious at first: he says that he had for years rarely eaten meat or used coffee or tea, "not so much because of any ill effects which I had traced to them, as because they were not agreeable to my imagination." This is a little less mysterious when we notice the emphasis he places on the "filth" and "ill odors and sights" that animal food brings into one's home and tells us why he speaks with authority of a sort: "Having been my own butcher and scullion and cook, as well as the gentleman for whom the dishes were served up, I can speak from an unusually complete experience." A full consciousness of all that is required by the eating of meat eventually results in repugnance, though it may take a while for it to do so. (See 493.23–5 and 33–3.) If vivid, first-hand knowledge of the operations that are involved in preparing animals to be eaten by humans would disgust you so much that you could not eat them, then you *should* be disgusted and shouldn't eat them. Similarly, he could say that the impersonality of the mechanisms by which we carry out our philanthropy merely masks from us the true nature of what it is doing. The features of the philanthropic relationship that inspired these poor families to reject Thoreau's help are still there in the event that the relationship becomes less personal. The impersonality is merely a matter of averting our gaze from these features, whatever they are. And they may well be something that marks the relationship itself as a way of connecting with people that is flawed or deficient, one that we have reason to try to avoid.

Two other arguments that Thoreau aims against the current high valuation of philanthropy reflect an approach to the subject that might be called "psychological." One of them presents his view of the psychological source of this overvaluation:

> Philanthropy is almost the only virtue which is sufficiently appreciated by mankind. Nay, it is greatly overrated; and it is our selfishness which overrates it. A robust poor man, one sunny day here in Concord, praised a fellow-townsman to me, because, as he said, he was kind to the poor; meaning himself. (382.36–383.1)

To grasp the plausibility of this argument, it is important to see the precise nature of the phenomenon he is trying to explain. It is the fact that the trait the he is calling "philanthropy" is almost the only one that people in our culture speak of as a virtue at all. A virtue is any trait that contributes to making a person a good person—as distinct from traits that make someone good in some more limited respect, as, for instance, ones that make one a good dentist or a good mathematician. If you ask almost anyone to name a person who strikes them as "a good person," the answer is virtually without exception some person who is remarkable for their philanthropic activities. Mother Teresa is the name that comes up with the bland inevitability of a cliché. Thoreau refers to the same sort of phenomenon when he quotes a learned lecturer listing the greatest "worthies" of England, the "greatest of the great": "They were Penn, Howard, and Mrs. Fry" (383.8–9).[9] This is what happens if you ask for examples of virtuous people. If you ask for examples of *traits* that make a good person, you get very much the same sort of result. The answers are almost always either identical to Thoreauvian philanthropy or very closely related to it: charity, compassion, caring, and so forth.

This is a very curious set of facts, one that requires an explanation. Consider, for comparison, the first great answer in Western philosophy to the question of which traits are virtues. This is Plato's list in *The Republic*: wisdom, courage, temperance, and justice. None of them is even close to philanthropy (or caring, and so forth). The next great list in the Western tradition, Aristotle's much longer one (it includes thirteen traits rather than four), also lacks a trait that is at all close to the one that Thoreau is talking about. It is true that Aristotle talks at length about generosity or liberality (*eleutheriotês*) but, as I will argue in a moment, this is a very different trait from philanthropy. These are the views of two of the wisest heads that have ever considered the question of which traits are to be regarded as virtues. The great difference between our pre-reflective judgments and the considered judgments of these philosophers needs to be explained. Part of the explanation is of course a matter of the history of ideas. Later philosophers, unlike Plato and Aristotle, do recognize philanthropy, or something like it, as at least one of the virtues. St. Thomas Aquinas makes Christian love, of which philanthropy is one component, one of his seven cardinal virtues. We see similar things in later lists of virtues put forth by moral philosophers. But this is still a long, long way from thinking that Mother Teresa or John Howard is the greatest of the great. There is still much to be explained. Thoreau's point of course is that part of the explanation has to be that we admire philanthropy because we want some of its help for ourselves. Our hyperbolic overvaluation of philanthropy is motivated by selfishness. But if philanthropy is the whole of virtue, or the greatest of virtues, then this sort of motivation is morally bad. According to its own constitutive moral standards, the extreme valuation we place on philanthropy is itself morally bad.

The other argument that could be regarded as psychological concerns, not the way we value philanthropy, but the psychology of the trait itself. Referring again to Robert Howard, the English prison reformer, he says, "Howard was no doubt an exceedingly kind and worthy man in his way, and has his reward; but, comparatively speaking, what are a hundred Howards to us, if their philanthropy do not help us in our best estate, when we are most worthy to be helped?" (381.26–31). He never defines what he means by philanthropy, but what he is saying here is intelligible if we suppose that what it consists in is remedying sufficiently serious deficiencies. Hunger is a serious deficiency, which is remedied by feeding the hungry person. Similar things can be said of poverty, weakness, ignorance, unhappiness, and so forth. They are ills that need to be remedied, gaps that need to be filled up. The problem he is raising here has to do with the fact that, while such deficiencies are not moral failures, they are certainly bad things. As long as we are acting philanthropically, we are responding to the deficiencies of others and not to things about them that have positive value. To grasp more fully what this means, consider the difference between philanthropy and two other virtues that have to do with pursuing the good of others: justice and generosity. In justice, a certain sort of justice at any rate, one is responding to the excellence of others with commensurate rewards and recognition. In generosity, one responds to others, not in terms of deficiencies to be filled up, nor yet in terms of virtues that require a response, but as an opportunity to do something positively good.[10]

Three more arguments against the common view of philanthropy rest on a theme in Thoreau's ethics that, as I have suggested, has so far only lurked in the background of my comments. It is sounded near the beginning of the philanthropy discussion: "Men say, practically, Begin where you are and such as you are, without aiming mainly to become of more worth, and with kindness aforethought go about doing good. If I were to preach at all in this strain, I should say rather, Set about being good." (380.31-3). Here he is setting out a fundamental feature of his ethical position. His ethics are basically an instance of what is often nowadays called "virtue ethics."[11] That is, while other ethical systems are best expressed in terms of rules about what actions you should do or avoid doing, this one is most perspicuously expressed in terms of what sort of person you should be. Since the ideal type of person is traditionally described in terms of what virtues they would have, the designation of "virtue ethics" is an appropriate description of the point of view that emphasizes this sort of issue.[12] His ideal is about who to be and not so much about what to do. To some extent, in making this statement, he is also specifying what the real target of his polemic is. The idea that he is attacking is the idea that the highest ethical good is to do philanthropic *actions*.

What sort of difference does it make, whether we think of the ethically good as a matter of what to do or of what to be? Why should we care? We can see one reason for caring by looking at two (or possibly three, depending on how we interpret them) of the objections to the philanthropy point of view that arise out of Thoreau's preoccupation with virtue. The first is so closely related to the virtue-ethical idea that it barely qualifies as a separate argument. It consists of an observation that philanthropy is a completely different kind of thing from what (according to virtue ethics) ethical value must be like:

I want the flower and fruit of a man; that some fragrance be wafted over from him to me, and some ripeness flavor our intercourse. His goodness must not be a partial and transitory act, but a constant superfluity, which costs him nothing and of which he is unconscious. This is a charity that hides a multitude of sins. (383.18–23)

If the philanthropy idea is right, then ethical goodness is an *episode*, something that happens intermittently, that punctuates life. According to the virtue-ethical approach the greatest ethical value cannot be a mere episode. It must be a *state* that a person is in, constantly.

Which of these two views should we take? Is the ethically good an episode or a state? Thoreau is suggesting a reason for preferring the latter one: If the good that we realize in our lives can be either an episode or a state of being, wouldn't the latter be *better* than the former? After all, it is always there, a constant, radiant presence. To aim at a sort of value that is a mere intermittent episode is to set your sights lower than need be. Such a good is not good enough.

There is another interesting idea in this passage. It relies on another feature of the virtue tradition, one that, we will soon see, is very important for his ethics. This is the idea that there is a deep connection between virtue and happiness. In the view of virtue theorists like Aristotle, a virtue, such as courage, generosity, or self-control, has an inside and an outside. The outside is the behavior that we can see. The inside is an established point of view about what is important and worthwhile, a settled inclination, and a range of typical emotional responses. These are what result in the consistent action that characterizes the virtuous person. Good people act as they do because this is what their view of the good, their inclinations, and their emotions lead them to do. This would explain why Thoreau says that the goodness of the good person "costs him nothing." Anything less that this would be unnatural and not what they wanted. Similarly, in "Civil Disobedience," in speaking of the possibility of breaking laws that require him to do things that depart from the path of virtue, he says, "It costs me less in every sense to incur the penalty of disobedience to the State than it would to obey" (215.28–30). Emerson expressed much the same idea when he said, "It is as easy for the strong man to be strong, as it is for the weak to be weak."[13] Good conduct is just what comes most naturally to a good person.

Thoreau bases another objection to the overvaluation of philanthropy on the foundation of this idea, that virtue leads to happiness. He compares two views of human beneficence by presenting, as an analogy, two ways of viewing the beneficence of the sun:

As if the sun should stop when he had kindled his fires up to the splendor of a moon or a star of the sixth magnitude, and go about like a Robin Goodfellow, peeping in at every cottage window, inspiring lunatics, and tainting meats, and making darkness visible, instead of steadily increasing his genial heat and beneficence till he is of such brightness that no mortal can look him in the face, and then, and in the meanwhile too, going about the world in his own orbit, doing it good, or rather, as a truer philosophy has discovered, the world going about him getting good. (380.35–381.5)

In this little allegory, he imagines the sun benefitting those around it, or trying to, in two very different ways. The first involves trying to deliberately bring about specific effects on others. The other involves becoming better and affecting others by means of one's own example—the world goes around him, becoming good. If it is true that virtue brings happiness in its wake, then the greatest beneficial effect you can have on others may be the rather nonspecific one of helping them to become better. And if the best way to do *this* is by one's own example, then simply being good may be the most genuinely beneficent sort of life you can live. Further, I believe Thoreau does think that true happiness only comes with virtue and that the best way to learn it is the example of others.

Of course, if you pursue this sort of beneficence rather than the other, you are in a way giving up your power to do good, since you really do not have much control over what use (if any) others will make of the example you provide, and having power to do good does mean having control. But in his rather humorous description of the other way the sun might undertake to benefit the world, he suggests that you didn't have this sort of power in the first place. The sort of effects you try to bring about "with kindness aforethought," as he puts it, don't often have the good results that you meant them to have.

But surely, we might object, there are good effects on others that we can deliberately bring about in just this way. If you are starving, I should feed you. That is surely an effect that is easy to bring about: that you are no longer hungry. Actually, this very idea is the basis of another of Thoreau's objections, one that sheds additional light on the difference between virtue ethics and its alternatives: "A man is not a good *man* to me because he will feed me if I should be starving, or warm me if I should be freezing, or pull me out of a ditch if I should ever fall into one. I can find you a Newfoundland dog that will do as much" (381.22–6). Obviously, he is not against philanthropy, nor is he even denying that, under the proper circumstances, you might have a hard obligation to rescue someone in need. "Rescue the drowning," he tells us, "and tie your shoestrings" (384.18–21). He is denying that such an obligation implies an ethically important virtue. "If you should ever be betrayed into any of these philanthropies, do not let your left hand know what your right hand does, for it is not worth knowing" (384.21). The reason he is giving here for that harsh judgment is one that flows naturally from the point of view of virtue ethics. On that point of view, if we are considering placing a very high value on philanthropic acts, our thoughts must go beyond the acts to a contemplation of the person revealed in the act. What does the act reveal about the person that is especially good? To pull the drowning person out of the water is a mere physical act, one that can be done by a sufficiently large dog. I am reminded of a statement we often hear from people who are lauded for saving a life in an emergency: "I am not a hero." This claim often sounds, to me, to have that sound of sincerity. Why does the person not feel like a hero?

Of course, there is something *behind* the act, something that is beyond the capacity of a dog to achieve. There is the recognition of the moral necessity of the act. But how high above the canine level of excellence does this take us? The moral necessity here is real enough, everybody can see it. However, just because the necessity is so clear, the act of seeing this necessity is not among the higher and finer things of which humans are capable. Perhaps this is why a person who saves a life so often denies being a hero: Surely you could not have stood there and done nothing!

Such, so far, are the main arguments in Thoreau's critique of the popular hypervaluation of philanthropy. First, the poor, for the most part, wish to avoid this degrading "help" from us. Second, our extremely high valuation of philanthropy is itself selfish, resting on a desire to receive some of its help ourselves. Third, in practicing philanthropy we focus on the deficiencies of others and not on their excellence. Fourth, philanthropy is partial and transitory, whereas real goodness is constant. Fifth, the greatest good we do for others is for the most part (unlike philanthropy) unintentional, consisting of the inspiring example of a life well lived. Sixth, the power over others that we try to exercise by more direct sorts of beneficence is partly or largely illusory. Seventh, giving needed items to others, because it is something anyone can do, does not use the highest and most distinctively human capacities and consequently lacks an essential feature of the highest virtues: it is not highly admirable, in comparison to the others. I hope it is clear from what I have said that Thoreau's case against philanthropy is penetrating, coherent, and should be taken seriously.

There is, however, an eighth argument that is in some ways more important than any of those I have described so far. It logically ties some of the other seven together. This argument comes forth in a passage that unfriendly readers might merely pass by, thinking it is no argument at all but simply an immoralistic paradox: "You must have a genius for charity as well as for anything else ... Moreover, I have tried it fairly, and, strange as it may seem, am satisfied that it does not agree with my constitution" (380.11–15). This comment, despite the half-joking tone of it, is actually the other side of the idea behind the disclaimer I discussed at the end II.5. There, he claimed that, because each person must find and pursue his or her own way, others need not—in fact should not—follow Thoreau's way. Here, he is in effect pointing out the further implication of the idea that one must follow one's own genius: namely, *he* need not follow the philanthropist's genius, that it would in fact be wrong of him to do so.

This brings me, finally, back to the issue with which I ended the last section: Is Thoreau a genuine pluralist, or does his pluralism disappear when he turns to posing solutions to the problems of human life? Here the problem he is struggling with is that of the value of philanthropy. What is his solution? You might think that it is, simply, that no one ought to be a philanthropist. But that is actually not his solution at all. He is a consistent-enough pluralist to apply his pluralism in such a way as to limit his own attack on philanthropy. He actually insists that you ought to pursue the philanthropist's way, provided only that a philanthropist is truly what you are:

> Probably I should not consciously and deliberately forsake my particular calling to do the good which society demands of me, to save the universe from annihilation; and I believe that a like but infinitely greater steadfastness elsewhere is all that now preserves it. *But* [emphasis added] I would not stand between any man and his genius; and to him who does this work, which I decline, with his whole heart and soul and life, I would say, Persevere, even if the world call it doing evil, as it is most likely they will. (380.15–23)

One might call this a vitalistic *defense* of philanthropy. Of course, there is nothing incoherent or inconsistent with the position he is taking, despite the fact that it is both an attack and a defense of philanthropy. What he is attacking and what he is defending are different things. He makes the value of philanthropy relative to the genius of the individual who is living it. He defends philanthropy that is an expression of one's own genius. He attacks philanthropy as an exalted cardinal virtue that is strongly obligatory for everyone. Only the latter sort of idea is involved in the challenge to the "very selfish" project he is pursuing at Walden. His own genius is not a philanthropic one.

Now we should be able to see how the narrative of his personal project in *Walden* is meant to represent the good. Obviously, it is meant to present us with concrete instance of the good life, described in sufficient detail to convince us that the good is at least possible and can be achieved. It also shows us the process, intellectual and practical, by which he found his project. He does not ask us to imitate his way of life—he virtually asks us *not* to—but he does ask us to use his philosophical method. This method serves to ground human action without trapping us into accepting the conclusions he has drawn. It is meant, in fact, to liberate us from others: this includes, of course, the larval tyrant that lurks within Henry David Thoreau himself, as it does in many of us.[14]

As you may recall, the reason I objected to Cavell's classifying *Walden* as an example of "prophetic" writing was this: to think of it that way implied that Thoreau feels that his words are actually the words of God and not the words of a particular, finite human individual. It seems to me, to the contrary, that Thoreau wishes us to be vividly aware, as we read him, of precisely which human individual is speaking, and of how close or distant he is to us, how analogous or disanalogous are our cases with his. Otherwise, we cannot estimate the relevance that his words might have to our own lives, and that is something he insists that we do. This may be one reason why he asserts, at the very beginning of the book, that "it is, after all, always the first person that is speaking" (325.24). That of course is a sentiment with which Jeremiah and Isaiah would have profoundly disagreed. This fact indicates a very deep difference between his sort of writing and theirs. He speaks only for himself, no one else, and bids you to do the same.

7. "Civil Disobedience" in the Context of *Walden*

We are now almost in a position from which we can turn again to the central argument of "Civil Disobedience," a subject I abandoned at the end of II.1. There is one thing still missing before I will be able to return to it, however. The missing element is an idea that, as a matter of fact, was already implicit in some of my comments on Thoreau's discussion of philanthropy. One point at which this idea indistinctly appeared was in my account of his pluralism. I said that he takes his vitalism to imply that his practicing philanthropy, given the peculiar nature of his own genius, would be a bad thing for him to do. He is applying the same reasoning to his non-philanthropy that he applies to his partial withdrawal from the economy. Just as it would be wrong and bad of him to plunge headfirst into the world of commerce, so (and for the same reason) it would be wrong and bad of him to practice philanthropy. There is a feature of subjecting both commerce and philanthropy to this sort of reasoning that will strike some as curious. For most of us, the question of the value of philanthropy is an ethical issue while that of the value of commerce is not. The question of whether I should practice philanthropy, we generally suppose, is settled by moral principles and ideas, while the question of whether I should go into business is a matter of personal fulfillment: it is a matter of whether I would find happiness by doing so. The notion of following one's own genius might be helpful for understanding what personal fulfillment is, but it does not seem so helpful for understanding what virtue is. Thus, while it might be relevant to (supposedly) nonethical issues like that of the value of commerce, how can it be relevant to a moral one like the value of philanthropy?

The answer is, I think, suggested by one or two things I have already said in my discussion of Thoreau's virtue-ethical critique of philanthropy, as well as my treatment in the preceding section on his vitalism. It is that this notion of following one's genius is not merely a formula for happiness but for virtue as well. A life that does not follow its own genius is not really a virtuous one. This is why he thinks that the fact that not everyone has a genius for philanthropy is relevant to whether it is a universal virtue.

The fact that the idea of genius grounds Thoreau's conception of virtue as well as his conception of happiness serves to explain why he makes the assumptions that underlie his arguments against philanthropy. If it is true that virtue is finding and following one's own genius, then for Thoreau it would follow that it is no easy task, involving a process of discovery and overcoming constant temptations to take the easy way out and follow the crowd. This would mean virtue is, as indeed he assumed in the seventh argument, an achievement that involves some of the higher capacities that are distinctive of human beings. The same fact also helps to support the virtue-ethical argument (the fourth one) that rests on the claim that virtue is continuous, not an intermittent episode. Living the sort of life that conforms to one's inner nature (again, given the way Thoreau understands it) is more like a state one is continuously in rather than an event. Further, if we suppose that following one's genius is a formula both of virtue and of happiness, then it follows immediately that virtue will bring happiness, because they are the same thing. It is no wonder, then, that Thoreau thought (as he argues in the sixth argument) that a life well lived is the greatest good we can give to others, in that it provides them with a clue to something that is of inestimable value *to them*. Finally, an ethic that focuses on virtue naturally tends to bring with it a certain conception of justice, according to which the strongest claim to our favorable attention is the possession of a virtuous character. A conception of virtue that more or less identifies it with flourishing (as Thoreau's does) would have a further implication: that a morality that focuses on providing remedies for our deficiencies thereby lavishes favorable attention on us precisely when we are least "worthy to be helped," as he maintains in the third argument.

The conception of virtue I have attributed to Thoreau will seem counterintuitive to many people, but it flows naturally from the argument for vitalism that I set out in II.5. This was the argument that, given his conception of human life as centrifugal, together with the assumptions that life is good and that whether we satisfy this conception is to a significant extent a matter of choice, it follows that life is a standard of value. But what sort of value is this? If it is true that life is a good thing and that its nature is such that one can move closer to, or fall further away from this good state, then it would seem that falling away from it amounts to entering a comparatively degraded state of being. To move in the opposite direction would be, by the same token, to enter an elevated state. To do either of these things as a result of one's own voluntary action would then be either admirable or the reverse of admirable. It makes sense to think of such a state as constituting virtue. In that case the value involved here is ethical value.

The central argument of "Civil Disobedience" is squarely based on this same line of reasoning, including of course this passage:

> The mass of men serve the State thus, not as men mainly, but as machines, with their bodies. They are the standing army, and the militia, jailers, constables, *posse comitatus*, &c. In most cases there is no free exercise whatever of the judgment or of the moral sense; but they put themselves on a level with wood and earth and stones, and wooden men can perhaps be manufactured that will serve the purpose as well. Such command no more respect than men of straw, or a lump of dirt. (205.20–6)

Viewing this language in the context of *Walden*, it is clear that he means it more or less literally: not that the people who behave this way have actually become wood or stones but that, through their own voluntary action, they have entered a degraded state, the condition of human beings who have given up the distinctively human form of life.

This idea is reinforced by another one, which also runs throughout "Civil Disobedience." He persistently suggests that the state which he attacks, together with the servants who do its bidding, are committing a sort of ontological error. He comments that the jail, with its walls and gratings, "treated me as if I were mere flesh and blood and bones, to be locked up" (216.18–19). He says that the people who put him in it are like boys who, "if they cannot come at some person against whom they have a spite, will abuse his dog" (36–7). Unlike the boys in question, however, they do not intentionally attack a surrogate victim; they merely mistake the surrogate for the original. Their mistake is about the *type* of being he is. They think he is a body.

This mistake is to some extent inevitable, given the nature of the state: "The State never intentionally confronts a man's sense, intellectual or moral, but only his body, his senses. It is not armed with superior wit or honesty, but with superior physical strength." This is why, as he says, "the state is half-witted" (216.37–217.4). Of the two parts of Thoreau's nature, it selects and deals with the wrong one, the one that is not essentially Thoreau.

Clearly, this is meant as an ontological claim, both about the individual and about the state. As to the state, it is perhaps obvious what Thoreau means: The state is distinguished from other human agencies by the fact that it has those walls and gratings, as well as many more brutal means, at its disposal. It only acts *as* the state, as opposed to acting as a preacher, a teacher, a debating society, a business corporation, or a club, when it uses or in some way threatens to use such means. As to the other side of this claim, the position it takes regarding the individual, it might also seem obvious what Thoreau is thinking: that the individual is more than anything else a spiritual being, a soul, and that this is why the actions of the state will always be in a certain way beside the point for beings like this.

From reading *Walden*, we can see that he has a specific conception of what the spirituality of the individual amounts to and of why this indicates that the action of the state is at best beside the point. The spiritual aspect of the individual human being is a certain form of life, in which one follows what he calls in *Walden* the indweller or one's genius. In "Civil Disobedience," with its strongly ethical focus, he calls the same aspect of one's life one's "conscience" and one's "moral sense." The working of the state tends to be inimical to the human spirit, not merely because it deals with human beings on the most crudely physical level, confining it with walls and gratings or threatening it with physical injury, but because it relates to individuals literally as *subjects*. That is, it requires people to subject their judgment to it by accepting it as their authority on matters of right and wrong. Subjecting oneself in this way, however, means making the fatal choice Thoreau has warned us against, of degrading oneself into a mechanism. This means that, when the state on the contrary commands you to collaborate with it in doing wrong, then you must disobey its command. This of course is Thoreau's celebrated method of civil disobedience, the use of disobedience as a means of bringing about social change.

III

Knowing Right from Wrong

1. The Voice of Conscience

You could say that Thoreau thinks that your life depends on your using your own judgment. Not in the sense that using your wits enables you to survive, though, of course, that is also true; rather, his idea is that, if you do not act on your own judgment, you are dead already. Quite literally, if you value your life, you must follow the promptings of your inner self.

This idea helps to ground one of Thoreau's most characteristic philosophical positions: his ethical intuitionism. In ethics (more exactly, metaethics), intuitionism is the theory that we can know ethical truths by means of unmediated (in the sense of non-inferential) awareness. That is, one can know some ethical truths without drawing them as a conclusion from any other truths. Here an objection immediately suggests itself. If you know something, then that thing must be true. And if Thoreau's vitalism is correct, then it does seem to follow that you ought to act on the pronouncements of your conscience, since the only alternative is a sort of death. But this has no obvious connection with the *truth* of what your conscience tells you. The Thoreauvian reasons why you should follow your conscience are about the nature of your self. However, if your conscience tells you that the institution of slavery is unjust, then if that is true, it would have to be because of the nature of slavery and not because of facts about yourself. Only if you accept solipsism, the idea that your self is the whole world, would intuitionism follow from vitalism. How then can intuitionism, a claim about how we can know the truth, follow from Thoreau's vitalism?

I think that we can get at least a partial answer to this question by making a distinction between intuitionism proper and what might be called methodological intuitionism. Methodological intuitionism is the notion that one ought to act *as if* ethical intuitionism were true. This I think does follow from his vitalism. If one accepts it without amending or qualifying it in some way, his vitalism does commit Thoreau to the notion that one should sometimes act as if it is possible to simply "see that" certain things are right or wrong, good or evil, not as a result of ratiocination, but as a result of having the right sort of insight. This I think would justify at least a good part of what he is trying to do in "Civil Disobedience."

There, he says,

> When I meet a government which says to me, "Your money or your life," why should I be in haste to give it my money? It may be in a great strait, and not know what to do: I cannot help that. It must help itself; do as I do. It is not worth the while to snivel about it. I am not responsible for the successful working of the machinery of society. I am not the son of the engineer. I perceive that, when an acorn and a chestnut fall side by side, the one does not remain inert to make way for the other, but both obey their own laws, and spring and grow and flourish as best they can, till one, perchance, overshadows and destroys the other. If a plant cannot live according to nature, it dies; and so a man. (217.10–22)

Here he describes his relationship to the state, in which he refuses to do what it tells him to do, in the face of a threat of lethal force, as if he were a mighty oak shading out the sapling of the state. It is tempting to see these remarks merely as a facile paradox. Looking at them in light of what I have just been saying, however, we can see that there is more to them than that. He is also saying that just as the state, in trying to force him to do its bidding, is following its nature and doing what states must do, so in resisting injustice he is also following his nature—his true nature, the promptings of his conscience.

I think it is clear that Thoreau believes methodological intuitionism, and that he believes it partly because of his vitalism. However, there is a complication here. It is also clear that he believes ethical intuitionism proper, that he thinks intuitionism is true and not merely that we should sometimes act as if it is. I will eventually have to untangle these two threads in the fabric of Thoreau's thinking, but before I attempt to do so, it might be helpful to look more closely at his use of them.

Probably the most fully developed use of intuition is his defense of his vegetarianism in the "Higher Laws" chapter in *Walden* (493.31–496.14), which I discussed briefly in II.6. This is the one in which he says that he rarely eats meat because it is not agreeable to his imagination. He makes it fairly plain that this appeal to imagination is an appeal to intuition: "It may be vain to ask why the imagination will not be reconciled to flesh and fat. I am satisfied that it is not" (494.28–30). When he denies that he knows why his imagination cannot be so reconciled, he is declaring that he has not derived his adverse view of killing, butchering, and eating animals from some other idea, as conclusion from a premise. His assurance that this practice is something to be avoided does not rest on such grounds.

He cleverly attempts to enlist the reader's own intuitions on the side of his argument. He tries to get us to suspect that there is a certain excessiveness about our eating habits by, in effect, challenging us to explain a certain phenomenon: "Most men would feel shame if caught preparing with their own hands precisely such a dinner, whether of animal or vegetable food, as is every day prepared for them by others. Yet till this is otherwise we are not civilized, and, if gentlemen and ladies, are not true men and women." Why is it that I would feel shame in preparing for myself alone the lavish sort of meals that I prepare for guests? If I cannot find an answer that explains it away, then I ought to accept the shame as a veridical experience of the actual value of such indulgences. Of the same sort is the argument I referred to in II.6, in which he points out our distaste for the process (gutting, skinning, and so forth) that is essential for preparing animal food for the table.

At times, it is clear that the idea he is employing here is precisely methodological intuitionism:

> It is hard to provide and cook so simple and clean a diet as will not offend the imagination; but this, I think, is to be fed when we feed the body; they should both sit down at the same table. Yet perhaps this may be done. The fruits eaten temperately need not make us ashamed of our appetites.

Here the standard of conduct is to follow the promptings of one's inner self. He says this more or less explicitly in the following observation: "If one listens to the faintest but constant suggestions of his genius, which are certainly true, he sees not to what extremes, or even insanity, it may lead him; and yet that way, as he grows more resolute and faithful, his road lies."

Yet even here he indicates that his intuitionism is not purely methodological, with an almost casual aside to the effect that these suggestions of one's genius "are certainly true." As I have said, *truth* does not seem to be a value that a merely methodological intuitionism based on Thoreau's vitalism can promise to deliver. He also seems to connect his intuitionist method with another value that, it would seem, cannot be based on vitalism alone, namely, *universality*: "I believe that every man who has ever been earnest to preserve his higher or poetic faculties in the best condition has been particularly inclined to abstain from animal food, and from much food of any kind." The desire to preserve one's higher capacities results in inclinations to abstain from animal food that are universal, in that everyone who has these desires also has these inclinations. Thoreau's claim to universality presents a problem, the same problem as his claim to truth. Different people have different inclinations. Indeed, the idea that one person's genius is different from the next is the basis of Thoreau's pluralism about the good life.

Yet, clearly, he is both a pluralist and a universalist. There is nothing per se wrong with that, of course. I am a pluralist about some things (like whether butter pecan ice cream is preferable to chocolate ice cream) and a universalist about others (such as whether committing murder is preferable to not committing murder). This seems perfectly consistent to me. Thoreau's problem is that his universalism and his pluralism seem to have the same basis: the imperative that one must follow one's genius.

As a first step toward searching for a solution to these two problems, those of truth and of universality, we should notice that he does qualify his description of the inner promptings that yield truth. It is not just any suggestions of one's genius, but the "constant suggestions." Nor is it just any objections one is inclined to make to eating flesh, but "assured" objections. Maybe he is making some sort of distinction between different aspects of one's genius: one that yields universal moral truths about the world and another one that only concerns itself with whither the path of one's own life should lead. This is potentially relevant to solving the problems of truth and universality. He is not claiming universal truth for all of our intuitions nor for intuitions simply as such. There might be some special reason for thinking that the limited set of intuitions that he is talking about have some special claim to being believed and acted upon.

There is another way in which Thoreau seems to qualify his intuitionism, one that moderates his position in a similar sort of way. When he thinks of his inner promptings as giving us universal moral truths about the world, they seem to be limited to pronouncing on certain subjects. They do not seem to tell him about what is good or worthwhile—that, for instance, self-sufficiency is better than participating in the economy, or that sexual abstinence is per se better than marriage. They generally only tell him about what would be wrong of him to do. They issue moral constraints.[1]

The two great issues in "Civil Disobedience" to which Thoreau applies his conscience are those of slavery and of the Mexican-American War (1946–8). The war began while he was at Walden and eventually resulted in the invasion of Mexico and annexation of approximately one half of its territory. The question he poses in both of these issues is, What relationships, what connections between himself and these events, *must he avoid*? His answer to this particular question is sweeping. "How does it become a man to behave toward the American government today? I answer, that he cannot without disgrace be associated with it" (206.8–10). Here he is acknowledging a limit on his own permissible behavior. What is the principled nature of this limit? With what sorts of injustices must he refrain from associating himself? And what sorts of relationships count as being "associated" with them?

> If the injustice is part of the necessary friction of the machine of government, let it go, let it go: perchance it will wear smooth—certainly the machine will wear out. If the injustice has a spring, or a pulley, or a rope, or a crank, exclusively for itself, then perhaps you may consider whether the remedy will not be worse than the evil; but if it is of such a nature that it requires you to be the agent of injustice to another, then I say, break the law. Let your life be a counter-friction to stop the machine. What I have to do is to see, at any rate, that I do not lend myself to the wrong which I condemn. (211.21–30)

Here he considers three possible levels of involvement with injustices that are perpetrated by government. Only the third and most intense level of involvement invokes a strict duty on his part. This is the case in which you "become the agent of injustice to another," in which you "lend" yourself to the wrong that is being done. The sort of association he has in mind here, between yourself and the state, is something very much like the legal relationship between agent and principal. If I am planning on taking a trip in which I will be out of touch with civilization for an extended period, I may give you the right to draw money from my checking account in order to pay my bills and manage my financial affairs. Under those circumstances, certain actions of yours would count just as if they had been done by me. In particular, this is true of actions that change one's rights and obligations. An obligation-assuming act on your part, such as signing a check, creates an obligation of mine. This is an instance of vicarious responsibility, of being responsible for actions that are admittedly not one's own but those of another. Thoreau is saying that this idea, which obviously makes sense when applied to moral relations like rights and obligations, also applies to guilt. We must avoid associations with certain wrongs done by the state, ones that are such that those wrongs would otherwise count as if they were done by ourselves. If we fail to disassociate ourselves from these wrongs, we would be guilty of them, even though we did not do those things ourselves.

The moral intuitions to which he is appealing here do seem to be ones that we all have. Suppose that agents of the state are executing political prisoners and concealing their bodies in a mass grave. It is debatable whether you have an obligation to try to stop them, especially if doing so would involve substantial risks to your own life. "I am not the son of the engineer." But one thing seems to be beyond dispute: you must not, knowing what they are doing, give or sell them the ammunition with which they are committing their evil actions. No one would do that and then say, "Well, I didn't actually pull the trigger, nor did I give any of the orders, so I am not responsible for what they did." Obviously, knowingly supplying the gunman with his ammunition would make me vicariously responsible, if anything could. To Thoreau, it is obvious that, on any reasonable interpretation of the idea of vicarious responsibility, paying taxes that will then be used to annex half of Mexico or return escaped slaves to their "owners" makes you responsible for what they are doing. These are actions that I would not permit myself to do. He believes that, for the same reason, I should not "lend myself" to the same actions when done by others.

The idea of vicarious responsibility implies that certain moral intuitions that we all apply to our own conduct also apply to the state. In effect, these moral intuitions to some extent supplant the authority of the state's lawgivers. But it is important to keep in mind that the range of intuitions that have this sort of upstart authority is circumscribed. It is limited to constant and assured acknowledgments of moral constraints. In addition, the things he says about these ideas indicate, I think, that there is one more way in which the sphere of these authoritative intuitions is circumscribed. Both the issues to which he applies his ethical views in "Civil Disobedience" involve violations of the rights of others. This, at any rate, is the obvious reason why you and I would not permit ourselves to own slaves or plunder the legitimate territorial holdings of others. We would be violating their rights.

Whenever he argues in a way that involves intuitions that produce moral constraints, he is always either talking about a course of action that would violate rights or one that at least would violate what we might call "rights-like considerations." The reason for the qualification, "rights-*like*," is his remarks about the ethics of eating animal food. I have treated them as a particularly clear case of his use of moral intuition, and yet he does not treat the issue involved as a matter of rights. His normative position on this issue is that the people who aim most earnestly to develop their highest faculties are inclined to do without animal food, and that as the human race as a whole progresses it, too, will be more and more so inclined. Clearly this is not how he would talk if his objection to eating animals is that the practice violates the rights of the animals. If he thought that, he would demand, as he does of slavery, that it stop at once.

As I say, it helps to keep in mind that the sphere of intuition's authority is limited to pronouncing upon a certain range of issues. For instance, there is this startling pronouncement in "Civil Disobedience":

> But a government in which the majority rule in all cases cannot be based on justice, even as far as men understand it. Can there not be a government in which the majorities do not virtually decide right and wrong, but conscience? ... Must the citizen ever for a moment, or in the least degree, resign his conscience to the legislator? Why has every man a conscience then? (204.23–9)

At first look, this is a rather baffling thing to say. It seems to rest on an obvious confusion between the role of law and that of conscience. Law and conscience do not "decide right and wrong" in the same sense of those words. My conscience is a way of deciding what I will or will not do. Law is an instrument for deciding what everyone covered by the law will or will not do. Law is thus a way of deciding for others. Conscience cannot do this for the simple reason that no one on earth, other than I myself, has any reason to follow my conscience. But I don't think he is calling for the conscience to perform this particular function of the law, nor (necessarily and immediately) for this particular function of the law to come to an end. "I ask for, not at once no government, but at once a better government" (204.13–14). His concern here, the issue to be decided, is whether he will become responsible for violations of the rights of others. This includes not only owning slaves or sending escaped slaves back into captivity. It also includes becoming responsible, by means of his allegiance and his tax dollars, for the slaveholding and slave-catching activities of others. As far as this issue is concerned, Thoreau's position is clear-cut. The promptings of one's conscience, at least on those important matters about which it speaks with a clear and unmistakable voice, must be must be taken as authoritative as far as decisions about one's own conduct are concerned. The only alternative to granting it that sort of authority is a sort of inner degradation and death.

One clue to the meaning of the above-quoted, initially mysterious passage is a clause that I omitted from it, in the place marked by the ellipsis. It comes immediately after "in which the majorities do not virtually decide right and wrong, but conscience?" and says, "—in which majorities decide only those questions to which the rule of expediency is applicable." What are these issues, to which the rule of expediency is applicable? He gives one example in "Civil Disobedience," when he says, "I have never declined paying the highway tax, because I am as desirous of being a good neighbor as I am of being a bad subject" (219.31-3). Even if the state allocates too many resources to maintaining the highways, or not enough, he violates nobody's rights by paying it. Further, he believes, the only reason why an allocation might be too much or too little will be "expediency": that is, the interests of the people affected by it. For him, it is not a moral issue at all. More generally, he seems to think that the issues to which expediency applies include all of those that remain after we eliminate the options that would require the individual decision-maker to violate rights.

I say that I will need to untangle Thoreau's methodological intuitionism from his adherence to intuitionism proper because they clearly are very different ideas, with different implications. Some of the ideas that he uses his intuitionism to support may indeed be supported by one of these versions of it but not by the other. In deciding whether to agree with these other ideas, it may help to take note of which version of intuitionism is in play. This taking note is what I mean by untangling the two ideas. It will be part of my task in the next section, in which I will consider various possible objections to Thoreau's intuitionism and the moral and political uses to which he puts them.

2. Assessing Thoreau's Intuitionism

Thoreau's intuitionism, and the political uses to which he puts it, are liable to get objections from several different directions. One rather obvious objection I have already answered. This is the claim that by supplanting the authority of the law with that of conscience, he takes up a position that leads immediately and in all cases to anarchy, where anarchy means simply chaos—everyone following their own conscience with no external authorities and no external rules whatsoever. I have argued, on the contrary, that he is willing to accept external authority—at least the authority in a democracy, which is that of the people (*demos*)—in the realm to which the rule of expediency applies. He apparently thinks that this includes by far most of the issues with which a well-run liberal democracy concerns itself. His position does not require the immediate extinction of civil authority.

The answer to the above objection, as I have presented it, rests on my interpretation of the text and, of course, assumes that I have interpreted it correctly. Other potential objections are answered more directly in the text itself. Thoreau makes it fairly clear that he is aware of possible objections to his views and, in various ways, indicates the sorts of replies he is prepared to make to them. A glance through some of these indicated replies will show how far he has gone in anticipating these objections. It will give us some idea of how cogent and systematic his thinking actually is. I think some of his less sympathetic readers will be surprised and favorably impressed.

First, he is quite conscious of the fact that some critics will claim that one feature of his point of view is open to a certain obvious and absolutely fatal objection. In effect, these critics will say, he makes the individual's private conscience the standard that determines whether a law is to be disobeyed and a government resisted. Of course, private conscience is a standard quite distinct from that of the public good. Thoreau's standard can therefore result in actions that are detrimental to the community, considered as a whole. What the public good requires is that we accept the decision-making authority of the legislator and do what it says.

This objection attributes to Thoreau a position that is not his. As I have already pointed out, he does not substitute, quite generally, his own judgments for the rule of law. He can accept, within proper limits, a central decision-making authority, and he might even think that these limits are fairly wide, that they normally include most public policy issues.

This, however, is not a very profound sort of response to this objection. It doesn't address the deeper ethical and political issues it raises. The text indicates that Thoreau is prepared to make a response that goes much deeper. He would point out that, though this objection appears to express unvarnished common sense, it really does nothing of the sort. It rests on a certain theory, one that he always treats as the principal counter-theory to his own. He indicates what this theory is by quoting at a crucial point in the argument of "Civil Disobedience" the words of William Paley, one of the earliest explicit proponents of this counter-theory. An interesting reflection of the importance Paley's theory had for Thoreau can be found in the very title of his own essay. When it was first published, it was titled, not "Civil Disobedience," but "Resistance to Civil Government." This is very nearly an inversion of the title of the chapter in Paley's book from which he is quoting here: "Duty of Submission to Civil Government." Here is what he quotes Paley as saying:

> So long as the interest of the whole society requires it, that is, so long as the established government cannot be resisted or changed without public inconveniency, it is the will of God that the established government be obeyed— and no longer ... This principle being admitted, the justice of every particular case of resistance is reduced to a computation of the quantity of the danger and grievance on the one side, and of the probability and expense of redressing it on the other. (206.36–207.5)

The theory that lies behind Paley's comment, the counter-theory to Thoreau's own, is utilitarianism, which holds that rightness of an act (or rule) can be determined simply by taking the sum (or average) of its good and bad effects on everyone it touches. Paley is simply applying this theory to the practical problem with which Thoreau is presently concerned: the issue of whether to obey government or resist its authority. That is also true of the objection to Thoreau's approach that I have been just been considering. If we are to hand over our decision-making authority to the legislator, and the reason (the only reason) why we are to do this is that it is in the public good, this obviously means that the public good as a moral principle is more fundamental than conscience. But it also means, less obviously, that it is more basic than political and legal authority as well. The idea must be that the ultimate standard is maximizing the sum of everyone's good. This, once again, is utilitarianism.

Thoreau's immediate reply to Paley leaves no doubt about the vast distance that separates this utilitarianism from his own position:

> But Paley appears never to have contemplated those cases to which the rule of expediency does not apply, in which a people, as well and an individual, must do justice, cost what it may. If I have unjustly wrested a plank from a drowning man, I must restore it to him though I drown myself. This, according to Paley, would be inconvenient. But he that would save his life, in such a case, shall lose it. (207.6–13)

At first glance, this reply might well seem both extreme and dogmatic. A closer look indicates that it might well be neither of these things.

First, by pointing out the cases that Paley "appears never to have contemplated," he indicates that he thinks of Paley, and not of himself, as the extremist. Utilitarianism is the idea that "expediency," as he calls it, applies to all practical questions alike. Thoreau is not making a similarly sweeping statement: he is not saying that expediency never applies. He is merely saying what any nonutilitarian says, that the utilitarian carries expediency too far. As we have already seen, he thinks that there are cases to which it does not apply, as well as cases to which it does. Admittedly, his notion of how we can tell the difference between the cases to which expediency applies and those to which it does not is bound to be one that would offend a convinced utilitarian. As to what this notion might be, he has already suggested at least one feature it would have in his discussion of the proper limits of majority rule: "Can there not be a government in which the majorities do not virtually decide right and wrong, but conscience?—in which majorities decide only those questions to which the rule of expediency is applicable?"

(204.23-7). The idea seems to be that the rule of expediency must be excluded from that area within which, if the law acts, it will inevitably preempt the work of conscience in distinguishing moral right from wrong. One plausible way to interpret this, suggested by some comments I have already made (III.1) about the scope of Thoreau's intuitionism, is this: If the law asks me to do x, where x is something my conscience says is wrong, expediency is irrelevant to the question of whether I should do x. Further, the scope of this principle is limited to cases in which the action the law asks me to do would make me a party to a violation of rights, where this includes becoming the principal behind the agent who carries out the actual rights-violating procedure. Situations to which this principle does not apply may well be ones to which utilitarian considerations are very relevant. In that case, utilitarian considerations may even be the only relevant ones.

For the present, though, the point is that he distinguishes situations that are occasions for expediency from those that are not, while the utilitarian refuses to do so. Further, our earlier discussion enables us to see that his peremptory-sounding response to Paley is not the mere dogmatic assertion it might seem. We can see that his claim that "he that would save his life, in such a case, shall lose it" rests on a great deal that he has to say about the nature of human life, especially in *Walden*. In particular, he is relying on his idea that happiness is strongly connected with virtue. He takes it as obvious, and does not bother to say it in so many words, that a doctrine that requires us to do what we know to be unjust for the sake of expediency thereby violates the requirements of virtue. In his view, this means that it also clashes with the conditions of true well-being.

This idea of a close connection between happiness and virtue also forms the basis for his response to an objection that is nearly the opposite of the utilitarian one. Just as some would say that his view is inadequately supportive of the public good, others would claim that it is *too burdensome* to the individual, that it is too invasive of the individual good. Though he insists that his principle merely obliges us to break the law when that law requires us "to be the agent of injustice to another" (211.27), we have seen that he believes that, under certain circumstances, the simple act of paying one's taxes constitutes an injustice to another: to do so would be, he says, "violent and bloody measure" (213.35-6). Thus his principles will not infrequently require people to bring down on themselves the fury that states show toward tax-evaders.

He acknowledges in strong terms how onerous this appears to be. He imagines a reader objecting: "But, if I deny the authority of the State when it presents its tax bill, it will soon take and waste all my property, and so harass me and my children without end." His immediate comment is, "This is hard." The response he then gives to this objection raises, in a way that some philosophers would find confused, considerations based both on virtue *and* on happiness. He says that one will have to live simply and support oneself in a way that involves little use of cash, so the state will have little to seize and expropriate. After all, he says, in an unjust system, it is wealth and not poverty that is an occasion for shame. He then makes the remark, which I have already quoted, to the effect that it costs "less in every sense" to disobey than to obey and adds, as if to explain this remark, "I should feel as if I were worth less in that case" (215.8–30).

Some readers would be inclined to suppose that this passage shows that Thoreau simply suffers from ignorance of the deep difference between considerations of happiness and considerations of virtue. This ignorance, it might be said, leads him to offering the shamefulness of a course of action as one of its costs, whereas shamefulness and costliness are entirely different (and, in a way, opposite) things. The viciousness of stealing is a very different sort of thing from the fact that one might be caught and punished for it. It also seems to lead him into the error of supposing, in the last-quoted remark, that warning us that a certain course of action can cause unpleasant feelings of guilt constitutes a moral argument against it. Such unpleasantness, some would say, can only provide a basis for prudential arguments, not moral ones.

Thoreau rejects the dichotomous distinction on which such objections are based. In his terms, the "costs" of the alternative to disobedience do include the fact that one would be doing something shameful. A life that is characterized by such choices is both more worthy of shame and less worthy of living than one in which one follows the voice of conscience. On such a view, the fact that something is shameful is just the sort of thing that could constitute a cost. He is describing these considerations as costs rather than as moral evils (which he believes he could do with equal truth) because that is the aspect of the truth that answers the present objection, which is that his recommended course of action is too costly.

Something similar might be said about the remark in which he offers his feelings of being worth less as reasons for thinking that obedience to an unjust law is costly. That is, we need to understand his comment in light of his views about the relation between virtue and happiness. He does not think that it is the *unpleasantness* of those feelings that speaks against obedience: such feelings would count, for him, because they would be based on an insight that the contemplated course of action would, by reducing one's own value, *thereby* reduce the value of one's life. Thoreau's method of civil disobedience is not merely a method. It is a means of bringing about change, of course, but it is more than that. In the circumstances in which it is genuinely required, the alternative to it is a sort of inner death. As this alternative is an intrinsic evil, so his method is not a *mere* method but good in itself. As such, it is good for the agent who uses it.

This feature of his method would probably also serve as a basis for his response to yet another potential objection to his position. This one would rest on the notion that his method, regarded as a purely political method—that is, as a way of influencing the state—seems entirely negative.[2] This, in fact, is often the way he himself describes it: "It is not a man's duty, as a matter of course, to devote himself to the eradication of any, even to most enormous, wrong; he may still properly have other concerns to engage him; but it is his duty, at least, to wash his hands of it" (209.23-6). This advice, that the citizen should "wash his hands" of evil—certainly not one of Thoreau's more happily chosen phrases—brings rather painfully to mind the conduct of Pilate, who was satisfied so long as his own moral cleanliness was left unsmirched by the crucifixion of Jesus of Nazareth. The obvious objection to such a policy would be that it can be fully carried out, can even achieve its goal, while the evil continues to exist; and, even if it brings the evil to an end, it does not cause something positively good to happen. "When the subject has refused allegiance," Thoreau says, "and the officer has resigned from office, then the revolution is accomplished" (214.1-3). It is not obvious how such a method can bring about the goal of most revolutions: the establishing of a *good* political system. Much less does it seem suited to bringing about the goal that he envisions at the beginning of the essay: namely, the ideal polity.

Thoreau's response to this objection would rest on the notion that, just as his method is an intrinsic part of the individual's good, it is also an intrinsic part of the political good. This is partly because, for an individualist like Thoreau, the goodness of the community is a function of the goodness of the individuals who are its members. Just as "a corporation of conscientious men is a corporation with a conscience" (204.34-5), so a polity of virtuous human beings is a virtuous polity. This effect does not require that everyone be virtuous, since the character of the group as a whole can be changed for the better if, to begin with, there are just one or two virtuous individuals: "It is not so important that many should be good as you, as that there be some absolute goodness somewhere; for that will leaven the whole lump" (207.32-5).

There is, however, a deeper reason why Thoreau is able to see his method as an intrinsic part of the political good. He does not view the process of civil disobedience merely as one of removing particular injustices, such as the Fugitive Slave Law or the Mexican War. He sees it as a political (and anti-political) process with much broader significance. It is, in fact, identical to the process he describes at the end of the essay (in a passage I quoted in II.1) as one in which individuals ripen and fall off the tree of the state.

In Thoreau's view, individuals who practice his method of civil disobedience stand outside the state. He speaks of members of the state (and not merely the victims of its violence, as are the Mexican and the slave) as *subjects*, and with equal consistency he speaks of the role of subject as consisting in subjecting one's own judgment about right and wrong in human conduct, across the board, to the enactments of the legislator. By this sort of reasoning, one who rejects this subjection to the state is not a member of it and so stands outside it. And this rejection is precisely the method of civil disobedience itself. It is true, as I said before, that he is willing to accept the decisions of the state in the contexts to which expediency applies. But he is the one who must judge, in his own case, where expediency applies and where it does not: this is the judgment that the state claims to make for him. It is this use of his own judgment that puts him outside the state.

Of course, such rejection does not take one outside the human community altogether.[3] There remain the bonds between individuals that Thoreau consistently describes in terms of neighborliness (see II.1).[4] Such language, in fact, pervades "Civil Disobedience."[5] In its twenty or so pages, the word "neighbor" and its cognates are used eighteen times. He refers to three specific individuals as neighbors of his, including Sam Staples, the jailor who arrests him. This language characterizes relations between individuals in ways that powerfully suggest normality and decency. Thoreau's depiction of Sam Staples's act of arresting him is calm and relatively matter-of-fact, but by the time that it occurs in "Civil Disobedience," he has built up a context of expectations in terms of which Staples's act seems to conflict jarringly with his role as his neighbor. Neighborliness represents some sort of moral constraint on the actions of individuals, including officers of the state.

It also represents a constraint on the conduct of those who disobey the state. This comes to the surface when Thoreau says he pays the highway tax because he is as "desirous of being a good neighbor" as he is "of being a bad subject" (219.31–3). More importantly, it is reaffirmed in the culminating passage on the ideal state that ends the essay, in which he says of the individuals who should be allowed to "live aloof from" the state that they have "fulfilled all the duties of neighbors and fellow-men" (224.21–3).

What is it to be a neighbor, in this sense of the word? It is a very different thing from being a subject, so different that Henry can be both a *good* neighbor and a *bad* subject. Of course, the two are connected in a negative sort of way: the requirements of being a good neighbor are liable to conflict with those of being a good subject. One relevant ethical principle that recurs in various different forms in "Civil Disobedience" is this: "If I devote myself to other pursuits and contemplations, I must first see, at least, that I do not pursue them sitting upon another man's shoulders. I must get off him first, that he may pursue his contemplations too" (209.27–31). This principle obviously states the barest minimum that neighborliness requires of us.[6] The refusal to get off the other person's shoulders would not constitute behavior that Thoreau would call neighborly—certainly not toward the exploited individual. The principle of minimal neighborliness, as it might be called, the idea that one must not ride on another's back, clashes in the present political context with Thoreau's role as subject, in that he can only be a good subject by violating it. That is because the legislator demands that he pay the expenses of an aggressive war against Mexico and that he return escaped slaves to their alleged owners.

In obeying the requirements of neighborliness, Thoreau believes that he is following his conscience. In his view, neighborliness, considered as a framework of constraints, is based on the promptings of one's conscience and, more generally, of one's genius. This idea explains the rather curious fact that Thoreau envisions at the end of "Civil Disobedience" a "more perfect and glorious State" (224.25-6) and yet describes this condition in a way that implies that it is stateless. If we take "state" to mean, not the coercive organization with which we are so familiar, but simply the fundamental fact of social order, or polity (*politeia*), then a "state" is exactly what he does describe here. The same idea can also explain the rather more curious fact that he imagines the possibility of a state—in the *coercive* sense of the word—that can "afford ... to treat the individual with respect as a neighbor," and not, of course, as a subject. This would mean, as he understands it, that such a state will allow people to "live aloof from it, not meddling with it, nor embraced by it," provided only that they live within the constraints of neighborliness (224.18-22). To many readers, it will seem incredible that any state could tolerate the principled rejection of its authority: it seems that it must move instantly, before such a fundamental offense leads to even worse mischief. What he has in mind, however, is not the mere rejection of subjection to the state; it also involves replacing such subjection with something else. His alternative polity, in which people are related as neighbors and not subjects and masters, is like the polity of subject and state in one respect: like the state, it includes a constraining framework of duties on which we may rely for public order.

The coercive state thus has no very good reason to punish those who reject it in this way. To do so is to "cry and resist before it is hurt" (211.6–7).⁷ Despite its machine-like characteristics, the coercive state is "not wholly a brute force, but partly a human force" (220.29–30) and is capable of learning that the principle behind Thoreau's sort of revolution actually carries out the same function that the coercive state claims to carry out: the creation of social order. This sort of learning is an essential part of an experimental process in which the old sort of order can be supplanted by a new sort: a glorious state, "the more perfect and glorious" for being no state at all.

3. Two Ways of Relying on Intuition

At this point, a distinction I earlier took some pains to make (III.1) becomes very important: namely, the distinction between intuitionism proper and mere methodological intuitionism. We have now seen Thoreau using ethical intuitions to deal with two radically different problems. One is the problem of whether he should do what the state tells him to do. The other is to create social order as, one enlightened person at a time, we drop out of the coercive state and thereby gradually create the more glorious one that will eventually supplant it.

In this section I will dig deeper into the assumptions behind Thoreau's treatment of these two problems. First, though, it will help if we first get a clearer view of some of the ways in which these two problems are different. The former one is practical in nature—it is a problem about what to do—and concerns the conduct of the individual decision-maker. Any time any one of us is commanded by the state to do something that seems wrong to us, we have precisely this problem: Should I do it or not? The latter sort of problem, on the other hand, does not call for any action from the individual decision-maker at all. This is partly because it is not practical but theoretical. It is not about what to do but what is so. More precisely, it is a prediction about what will be so, as we gradually drop out of the state one at a time. Beyond that, it cannot be an occasion for action of my own because it is not about me as I contemplate the problem but about the social order that is to emerge with time as many people, over whom I have no control, make their own decisions. What will society be like in the future, if certain things happen in the meantime? It is not for me to decide what people in general will do in the future.

Thoreau's solution to the former problem seems to follow rather obviously from his methodological intuitionism. *If* we ought to act as if our constant and assured intimations of moral constraints on our behavior are true, then clearly when the state orders us to violate those constraints we ought to disobey it. Matters are apparently quite different for the second sort of problem. This is so, in the first place, because the problem one is contemplating here is not about what one ought to do. That, in fact, *is* what the principle of methodological intuitionism is about. That principle is consequently irrelevant to this problem. But the irrelevance is actually deeper than this. It is also irrelevant because of the nature of the principle itself.

The second problem is about the possibility of social order in a society of neighbors, in the absence of a coercive state. In order to achieve this sort of order, we would need principles of social order, which, like the law, tell different people the same thing. This does not mean that it must treat everyone exactly the same. A principle of social order can say that I have a right to withdraw money at will from a certain bank account and you do not. But if it says that I may do so, it must say that to me, to you, and to anyone else who consults it. If it says that you may not take the money, it must say the same thing to all who will listen. Otherwise, the fact that you and I are faithfully following the same principle will not prevent us from coming into conflict. This would seem to mean that it requires the sort of universality that mere methodological intuitionism cannot deliver. As we have seen, not only do different people's consciences seem to tell them different things, but Thoreau's own doctrine, insofar as it treats the voice of conscience as an aspect of the promptings of one's genius, could be interpreted as *predicting* that this would be so. After all, each person's genius is very different. You and I might follow the same principle—that is, the promptings of conscience—and yet still come into conflict. We can hope to avoid this conclusion if we can suppose that intuitionism *proper* is true. The truth that the genuine intuitionist believes we can get by means of unmediated awareness is the same for everyone and available to all, if they will only consult it.

So far, our examination of these issues yields the impression that full-blown intuitionism is needed to back up Thoreau's position on the problem of stateless social order but does not seem to be needed for his solution to the problem of whether to obey the state. What I would like to suggest in the rest of this section is that this impression is actually wrong. Intuitionism proper does *not* help him on the social order problem but *will* serve to make his position on the other issue, that of whether to obey the state, more plausible.

I will take the social order problem first. The reason intuitionism proper seems to help here is that it predicts that the voice of conscience could at least in principle be something that tells everyone the same thing—provided only that the practical problem under consideration is one about which conscience does have something to say (it is not merely a matter of expediency). Without the assumption of intuitionism proper, Thoreau's solution to the problem of social order has no plausibility at all. With it, one might think, there is at least a hope of its being plausible. Intuitionism is of course a perfectly respectable philosophical theory.[8] But like any philosophical theory, it is controversial: just as some people find it compelling, others find it implausible. I won't be able to explore the issue of its ultimate adequacy as an account of moral knowledge here. But I will say a few words to the effect that intuitionism, even if true, is not sufficient to support Thoreau's solution to the social order problem.

The reason is that even if the intuitions that the intuitionist believes in—insights that yield truth and universality—exist, they do not seem to be the sort of thing that could perform the function of a legal system. Consider the example I just used, of my alleged right to make withdrawals from a particular bank account, say the one bearing my name in the Plumas Bank of Portola, California. There are a great many ideas and principles that you and I must agree on in order to avoid coming into conflict over my right to make a withdrawal. Obviously, we must share the idea of property and some closely associated principles about the wrongness of taking the property of others, and about the right of the owner to make various uses (which ones?) of the items in question. Some of these are ideas that we might perhaps agree about simply on the basis of independently arrived-at intuition. Once we have accepted the idea of property itself, it might then be true that the idea that stealing it is wrong is self-evident (known non-inferentially) and would seem to be so to everyone who accepts the idea. This is what intuitionists would probably predict, and so far their theory does have a certain plausibility. However, for many other relevant ideas it is impossible to imagine arriving at agreement by these simple means. What if I claim that I have a right to this money because I inherited it from my father, while to you the practice of inheritance seems unjust? What if you and I are siblings, and Dad died intestate: Who gets his bank account then? What if I accept the principle that Dad's clear wishes ought to be carried out—and I believe that he clearly would have wanted everything to go to me? Mightn't you think that everything should be divided equally among us? And who counts as "us"? If you presented your idea to me, could you count on my changing my mind and agreeing with you? These issues are a very small indication of the number and complexity of the ones that can, and eventually will, arise in situations like this one, as anyone who has read cases in the law of property will know.

One might think that, if Henry's ideas were followed, life would be much simpler than it is now, so that people would have no such complicated issues to disagree and fight about. Maybe there would be no banks or bank accounts. Perhaps there would not even be any money. This, however, does not seem to be compatible with the pluralism that I have been attributing to Thoreau. Most likely, those who find their encouragement and inspiration in precisely the present state of things—and, as I will show later, he does admit that they exist—will, even if they truly follow their own geniuses, live the sorts of lives that will generate this sort of complexity. *They*, at any rate, will need money, banks, and bank accounts. Further, the particular issues that I have just described, all of them, would just as likely arise from ownership of a plot of farmland as they would from ownership of a bank account. And I doubt it will be argued that Thoreau's philosophy would do away with agriculture or private property in agricultural land.

Intuitionism makes the most sense if we restrict its scope to the most basic moral principles and definitions. Ideas like "it is wrong to take the property of others" or "promises ought to be kept" might conceivably be self-evident once we understand them. However, the idea that individual intuition could provide the foundation for basic social order requires that the scope of intuition go very far beyond this extremely limited territory, supporting a virtual infinitude of points at which our conduct would have to be coordinated. The idea that it can do so, I am very sorry to say, is just not plausible.

Of course, there remains the possibility that Thoreau is not committed to this implausible view. After all, he does not speak, in so many words, of "independent intuitions" in this context. That was my way of making sense of the things that he does say. There are no doubt other plausible ways to provide for basic social order. However, at the end of "Civil Disobedience," he does clearly represent the transition to a stateless order as a process in which individuals act entirely on their own, in which individuals drop off the state like fruit dropping off a tree, after they as individuals have attained the sort of maturity that is apparently both necessary and sufficient for stateless order to arise. If what I have just been saying is true, then this cannot be the way such an order arises. The process would have to involve the creation of shared principles of action, the sort of principles that are embodied in legal systems. For that reason, the formation of such a social order would have to be a social process, not one that emerges when individuals do things on their own. This does not necessarily mean that such a social process is impossible without the coercive mechanism of the state, only that the way in which it happens would have to be quite different from the very natural way he depicts it as happening.⁹

My main point here, for the moment, is that while it looks at first glance as if Thoreau's full-fledged intuitionism can back up his very individualistic solution to the social order problem, it actually is unable to do so. The reason is that individual intuition, even if it does in some way provide the ultimate foundation of moral knowledge, is still ill-suited to the task to which he seems to be applying it. What about his solution to the other problem, of whether we should submit to the state when it commands us to do something that conflicts with conscience? Here, as I have said, his conclusion seems to follow from his principle of methodological intuitionism alone. On closer examination, though, there is a problem here as well.

This principle, as I am interpreting it, is based on a more basic principle: his vitalism. You ought to follow the promptings of your inner nature, including especially your conscience, because to do so is to be alive, which is good in itself. This, however, seems to mean treating your own internal constitution, and the resulting subjective opinions and judgments about things, as if they were the standard of truth about those things—even though the principle itself does not claim that what these subjective opinions and feelings tell you *are* true. In other words, it would justify us in treating opinions as true even when they are not.

To see why this is a problem, consider the case of someone whose conscience tells them something that (let us suppose for the sake of the argument) is not true. Suppose I find that the most persistent and assured promptings of my conscience inform me that it is my duty to bomb an abortion clinic, killing whoever happens to be inside. That such people do exist is unfortunately undeniable. There *are* terrorists. Would the principle of methodological intuitionism imply that such people ought to commit their murderous acts? Here I see an ambiguity. The principle, as I have just formulated it, does seem to have this implication. I have phrased it as stating quite generally a notion about what we should do. One should act *as if* ethical intuitionism proper were true. On the other hand, the fact that Thoreau has focused on the specific problem of what to do when the state commands you to do something you think is wrong suggests the possibility of a narrower interpretation: perhaps the principle should mean that one should follow one's conscience when someone is attempting to force one to do something *that violates it*. An even narrower interpretation would be as follows: one should follow one's conscience when it indicates that what someone is attempting to force one to do *would violate the rights of others*.

These narrower interpretations offer, at least on the face of it, a hope of avoiding the problem of the terrorist. The state is not, in any straightforward sense, forcing the would-be bombers to do anything, much less is it forcing them to do something they think is wrong or violates the rights of others. Rather, the state is trying to *prevent* them from doing something. Such people think that the acts that the state is trying to prevent are ones in which they would be preventing others from doing wrong (by killing the wrongdoers). They may think that they have an obligation to do such things. That would mean that (according to their view of the matter) by prohibiting murder the state is prohibiting them from doing their duty. But Thoreau explicitly denies that people have the sort of duty that they think they have: a duty to eradicate wrongdoing (209.23-4). So if either version of the narrow interpretation is true, then the position that Thoreau takes in "Civil Disobedience," if we take *all* of it into account, would not imply that the would-be bomber should bomb the abortion clinic.

However, the whole of what he says in "Civil Disobedience" is, in a way, irrelevant to this issue. The problem is whether a *certain* principle underlying his argument leads to the terrorist problem. If his position is that you have, under certain circumstances, a duty to disobey the state because you ought to follow the promptings of conscience, then he accepts a principle that seems to justify the acts of conscientious terrorists.

One way to avoid this problem would be, as I have hinted above, to avoid purely methodological intuitionism and adopt intuitionism proper. This would mean accepting a certain constraint on what will be accepted as the voice of intuition or of conscience: if a given opinion is not true or not universal, it cannot be backed by the authentic voice of moral intuition. If I hold this principle, and I am sure that the abortion clinic bomber does not have a genuine duty to do what they do, then I must conclude that in thinking that they do have such a duty, they are not following the promptings of conscience or moral intuition at all. They might think that they have these intuitions, but they are just wrong about that. Perhaps they are following the lead of some preacher or guru, or some other socially constructed source of opinion, but certainly not conscience. This obviously avoids the problem of the terrorist altogether. Thoreau is no longer committed by his theory to saying that, just because they think they are following the promptings of conscience, they ought to do what they do. His principle will require him, on the contrary, to say that, just because what they think right is *not* right, it is not the voice of conscience.

Of course, this approach to the problem requires one to accept a very substantial philosophical theory. Not everyone who sympathizes with Thoreau on the issue of obedience to the state is willing to accept this theory. One might well wish to hold on to the moderate view attributed to him by the narrow interpretation but without having to carry around the hefty intuitionist baggage: that is, to restrict the scope of his methodological intuitionism to circumstances in which one is forced to do what one thinks is wrong or violates rights. But there is a possibility that this tactic might be objectionably ad hoc. Is there any reason, other than the desire to avoid a counterexample, to restrict one's position in this way? If there isn't, then it may well be that the principle underlying the position, whatever it might be, may well commit one to the broader position, the one that is liable to devastating counterexamples.

Another way to put the same issue is this: Is being forced to do something that one thinks is morally wrong or violates the rights of another a *special case* of being forced to do something? Is it different from the other cases in a relevant way, in a way that might justify us in treating it this differently—so differently that in this case one has an obligation to disobey, while in the others one does not? Does this make sense?

As a matter of fact, it seems to me that it does. This idea is, at any rate, supported by a notion that most people believe. This is the notion that morally wrong acts (especially ones that violate the rights of others) are per se *worse than* the other wrong things that one might do and so more difficult to excuse. Now, if someone says that such an act is permissible, just because the state is forcing you to do it, what they are saying is that the state's force is enough to excuse what you would be doing. But this commonly accepted notion, that rights-violating actions are worse than other wrongs, implies that such actions are in a sharply different category from other cases of being forced to do something. It is at least plausible to say that it is obligatory to refuse to do such things, even though it is not obligatory to refuse to do anything else the state forces one to do. It may be that "the state made me do it" is never enough to excuse or justify such actions, even though it can be enough to excuse or justify actions that are bad in other ways. If the only reason to disobey is that obedience costs me more money than the alternatives, and brings me no offsetting benefits, or that it constitutes an inefficient use of highway funds, then obeying is an innocent act. On the other hand, if the reason to disobey is that the obedient act violates someone else's rights—if it asks me, say, to be a party to theft, enslavement, conquest, or murder—then perhaps the state's threats are not a good enough excuse.

So far, here is where we stand: neither sort of intuitionist principle, neither intuitionism proper nor its merely methodological counterpart, will support his favored solution to the problem of social order. His conception of the way a stateless society could arise is simply too individualistic. As to the problem of whether to obey the state: His solution to this is in a sense supported by mere methodological intuitionism alone, since it tells us to follow our conscience and, presumably, ignore orders that conflict with it. However, there is a problem with the principle itself. Understood in this way, it seems to run right into the terrorist problem, since it would imply that they ought to do just what they are doing, which seems clearly wrong. Is there a way in which someone who favors Thoreau's solution to the problem of whether to obey the state might be able to contain the implications of methodological intuitionism, so that it requires us to disobey the state in the sorts of situations that Thoreau is concerned with in "Civil Disobedience" and avoids the implication that terrorists have an obligation to violate laws against murder and mayhem? I have said yes, one can take the position attributed to Thoreau by the "narrow interpretation." Being forced to do something that you think is morally wrong (especially if you think it is wrong because it violates rights) is a very different matter from being forced to do something you think is wrong for other sorts of reasons.

4. The Problem of John Brown

Whether the narrow interpretation of the "Civil Disobedience" doctrine shields Thoreau against the terrorism problem depends partly on whether it is actually a correct interpretation. If it is not, then perhaps someone sympathetic with his views, some revisionist Thoreauvian, might be able to use it to avoid the problem, but it will not serve to protect the body of beliefs that Thoreau himself actually held. *Is* it correct?

The issue of interpretation is complicated by the fact that, a decade after he wrote "Civil Disobedience," dramatic events impelled him to write "A Plea for Captain John Brown." In that essay, he goes well beyond the position that the narrow interpretation attributes to him. The essay on Brown appears to be a passionate and unqualified endorsement of John Brown's methods, and those methods at times amounted to what we now call terrorism.

It is not clear whether Thoreau at that time knew of Brown's most violent acts. The most notorious of these was the Pottawatomie Massacre of Saturday, May 24, 1856. In reprisal for a murderous attack on Lawrence, Kansas, by proslavery gangs, Brown masterminded and led a raid in which he and six others took five proslavery members of the so-called Land and Order Party from their homes along Pottawatomie Creek in the middle of the night. Taking them some distance down the road, they hacked and stabbed them to death with broadswords. Though Brown did not participate in the stabbings, he apparently did shoot one of the victims, a certain James Doyle, in the head to make certain he was dead. The murderous attack was denounced as "barbarous" even by Kansas abolitionists at the time.[10] Whether Thoreau knew the details of this incident or not, he clearly did know the basic facts of the then-recent raid on Harpers Ferry (October 16–18, 1859), an incident for which Brown was awaiting trial. In it, as every student of American history knows, Brown and a small group of followers attacked a Federal military arsenal in order to capture weapons and spark a general slave rebellion. Thoreau must have known, at least, that Brown was responsible for actions that the government would regard as criminal homicide.

His pro-Brown argument in this late essay connects it in an interesting way with the intuitionism of "Civil Disobedience" and *Walden*. He does not, in so many words, offer the promptings of conscience as the standard by which Brown's actions are justified, but the things he does say are ones that an intuitionist would be likely to find appealing. His defense of Brown avoids making the sort of case that one would expect a defender of Brown to make. Above all, he does *not* do what we would expect a utilitarian to do: namely, look at the details of what Brown actually did and trace their consequences. Nor does he argue that Brown's actions are appropriate to their circumstances. Rather, he talks about Brown himself, saying, for instance:

> He was one of that class of whom we hear a great deal, but, for the most part, see nothing at all—the Puritans. It would be in vain to kill him. He died lately in the time of Cromwell, but he reappeared here. Why should he not? ... They were neither Democrats nor Republicans, but men of simple habits, straightforward, prayerful; not thinking much of rulers who did not fear God, not making many compromises, nor seeking after available candidates. (308.6–17)

In describing Brown, he repeatedly uses the phrase, "a man of." Brown is "a man of principle," "a man of great common sense," "... of Spartan habits," "... of ideas," "... of faith." Though he talks only about the sort of person Brown is, he means this as a justification of what he does. This, in effect, is a virtue-ethical defense of Brown: it is the sort we would expect from a proponent of virtue ethics. One particular feature of Brown's virtue that he treats as important is the fact that, as he sees it, Brown is acting on the basis only of the most persistent and assured promptings of his own conscience. Relying on memories of the one occasion on which he personally met Brown, he says this of him:

A man of rare common sense and directness of speech, as of action; a transcendentalist above all, a man of ideas and principles—that was what distinguished him. Not yielding to a whim or transient impulse, but carrying out the purpose of a life. I noticed that he did not overstate anything, but spoke within bounds. (399.12-17)

Whatever Thoreau thought when he was writing "Civil Disobedience," by the time of the crisis that gave rise to the John Brown essay he had arrived at a position that is more extreme than the one attributed to him by the narrow interpretation.

In a limited sort of way, he can still avoid the terrorist problem, even with the position he takes on Brown's violent activities. The bomber problem was that of whether he is committed to saying that the bombers ought to do what they do. Here he is not saying that Brown ought to have done what he did. He is still able to make a distinction that he makes in "Civil Disobedience," between a duty to eradicate evil and a duty to wash one's hand of it, and he can still say, as he did there, that there is no such thing as a duty to eradicate evil. What Brown did was not something that he had a duty to do. What he did, on Thoreau's view, was supererogatory: beyond the call of duty. But this would be to escape the problem on a technicality. After all, he clearly is saying that what Brown did was justified, though admittedly it was not something he positively ought to have done. But if he is saying, by implication at least, that Brown was justified by the fact that he acted on the persistent and assured promptings of conscience, then it would seem that he must say the same thing of the sincere (and is there any other kind?) abortion clinic bomber and many another who commits acts of terror in pursuing what they view as a noble cause.

Does this mean that his position is hopelessly confused? I don't think so. Certain aspects of his position are, I think, deeply problematic, but it is at least conceivable that we might untangle the problematic parts from the rest. The source of the problems I have tried to identify is, after all, *not* his idea that you sometimes have an obligation to disobey the state. The problems all stem from the intuitionist foundations that he endeavors to put under that idea. The assumptions underlying his defense of Brown seem to imply that anyone who acts on the persistent, assured promptings of conscience is justified. This is what raises the terrorist problem.

He could defend disobeying the state without running into that problem if he used some other set of basic principles. He could even defend Brown. For instance, he might build on a natural rights position similar to the one that John Locke sets out in the *Second Treatise of Government*.[11] He might say that human beings need certain rights in order to live together as rational beings who must produce what they need, often by cooperation. He could elaborate a core of fundamental rights that are needed if social cooperation between such beings will be possible. This would have to include rights of self-defense, and the defense of others, against violators of these rights. The function of law and the just powers of the state (if there are any) would have to consist in codifying and protecting such rights. A case might well be made, then, that Brown was defending slaves against the right-violating acts of their so-called owners. To make such a case, we would of course have to look at what Brown actually did, and try to show that it is appropriate to the circumstances—that is, that it is in proportion to the seriousness of the rights-violating acts that he was trying to defend against, that measures like his are reasonably necessary in order to accomplish this end, and so forth.

Obviously, this could easily lead to taking the sort of position that I was attributing to Thoreau in the "narrow interpretation" of "Civil Disobedience." However it might be spelled out in detail, I think my main point here is already obvious: this way of defending Brown would not even come close to justifying the morally evil acts of terrorists.

5. The Idea of the Neighbor in *Walden*

Let me return to the concept of the neighbor, this idea that seems to form the bedrock of Thoreau's notion of the good society, his foil, in "Civil Disobedience," for state coercion. Rather oddly, the passages of *Walden* that are most relevant to the notion of the neighbor in "Civil Disobedience" are not to be found in "The Village," which is about people who live close to one another, but in "Solitude," which is about living alone. Also relevant is the chapter that follows it, "Visitors," which is about contact with people who do *not* live close by. In a typically paradoxical move, Thoreau discusses the concept of the neighbor by discussing its apparent opposite—namely, geographic separation from others. His point is to show that these things are not really opposites after all.

The discussion in these passages revolves around something that, he says, people "frequently say" to him: "I should think you would feel lonesome down there, and want to be nearer to folks, rainy and snowy days and nights especially" (428.9–12). The comment is, almost word for word, identical to one of the questions that he tells us, in the second paragraph of the book, inspired him to write it in the first place. The complexity and subtlety of his response to this comment indicate that he takes it very seriously. I will only remark on one aspect of it here.

What is the opposite of loneliness? Presumably, it is a certain desirable state of being near people. But just what is the nature of this nearness? He disposes of the most obvious answer with some counterexamples: "What do we want most to dwell near to? Not to many men surely, the depot, the post-office, the bar-room, the meeting-house, the school-house, the grocery, Beacon Hill, or the Five Points, where men most congregate" (428.21–5). Supposing that the opposite of loneliness is a good thing, it cannot consist merely of the physical fact that other people are nearby, together with the natural psychological consequences of that fact. His own account of what it is has a distinctly mystical sound: "Nearest to all things is that power which fashions their being... *Next* to us is not the workman whom we have hired, with whom we love so well to talk, but the workman whose work we are" (429.4–8). This creative power, "the perennial source of our life, whence in all our experience we have found [life] to issue" is something that "will vary with different natures." Wherever this source might be, he says, "this is the place where a wise man will dig his cellar" (428.25–9). What he seems to be offering is a vitalistic (and, consequently, pluralistic) conception of what it is to be "close" to something or someone. The paradigm here seems to be the sense in which two people are said to be "close"—as in "Dad and Uncle Charlie were always very close." He is stating it in terms sufficiently general to apply the concept to entities other than people and, most especially, to nature. His proposal is that one is close to an entity to the extent that the entity enables one to live as the particular person that one is. On his view, if Dad and Uncle Charlie were close, this means that each contributed significantly to the other's development, that they grew together.

The state of being close to something is the same thing as being its neighbor. This, then, is Thoreau's account of what it is to be a neighbor, or an important part of it. According to it, the sort of space that prevents one from being in this state, that separates one from one's fellows, is not physical space at all. For lack of a better term, one might call it "ethical space," resorting to an ancient conception of the ethical, in which it has to do with the formation of individual character (what Aristotle calls *ethismos*).

Thoreau's development of the notion of the neighbor in "Civil Disobedience" is rather different from his treatment of it in *Walden*. The differences seem complementary, though, rather than contradictory. His treatment in *Walden* is a conceptual journey to a utopian island, where he finds what the role of the neighbor ideally is. He sees it functioning serenely and unmolested. In "Civil

Disobedience" Gulliver returns to the land of the Yahoos. There he finds the ideal existing, but in a thwarted form, and he examines some of the conditions that interfere with it. Consonant with the theory set forth in *Walden*, mere physical separation is not among the inimical conditions. What does separate people in the relevant sense includes aggression, slavery, and injustice in general. It also includes, to the extent that it promotes such injustices, the coercive state.

IV

Economy

1. A Problem: Nature and Asceticism

In the chapter of *Walden* called "Higher Laws" a certain perhaps unfamiliar aspect of Thoreau's thinking moves into the foreground:

> If the hunter has a taste for mud-turtles, muskrats, and other such savage tidbits, the fine lady indulges a taste for jelly made of a calf's foot, or for sardines from over the sea, and they are even. He goes to the mill-pond, she to her preserve-pot. The wonder is how they, how you and I, can live this slimy, beastly life, eating and drinking. (496.32–7)

More striking still is this passage:

> Chastity is the flowering of man; and what are called Genius, Heroism, Holiness, and the like, are but various fruits which succeed it. Man flows at once to God when the channel of purity is open. By turns our purity inspires and our impurity casts us down. He is blessed who is assured that the animal is dying out in him day by day, and the divine being established. (497.35–498.1)

It is certainly not obvious that we can reconcile this distinctly otherworldly strain in Thoreau with the fact that we so often find him celebrating physical nature, including apparently pure animality, including even the animal side of his own nature. Just a few pages earlier, he says, "Once or twice, however, while I lived at the pond, I found myself ranging the woods, like a half-starved hound, with a strange abandonment, seeking some kind of venison which I might devour, and no morsel could have been too savage for me" (490.6–10). Put this way, his affirmation of nature seems to be a mere mood or appetite, but it is usually much more than that: a tenet or principle he holds—or that has hold of him. As a principle, it seems to contradict his otherworldly side, which also seems to have the status of a principle of some sort.

I will call this otherworldly side of Thoreau's thinking his "asceticism." Asceticism, in this sense, includes any ethical code or principle that entails that the concerns most intimately connected with the physical basis of human survival are much less valuable and important than they are normally taken to be.[1] On this definition, asceticism includes ideas that devalue the activities of eating and drinking, and sex as well, since these are all essential for the survival of the species. It seems clear that, to one degree or another, Thoreau does adhere to asceticism in this sense of the word. The problem, then, is to see whether this aspect of his thinking can be reconciled with his other views about what is valuable or important. I propose to begin treating this problem by the somewhat unusual approach of compounding it. For there is another very pronounced sort of asceticism in Thoreau's writings, in addition to the one that is evident in the passages I have just quoted. It also raises a problem concerning the consistency of Thoreau's works. It is a different problem from the one I have already pointed out, but I will argue that the solutions, or partial solutions, of the two problems are essentially the same. I say "partial solutions" because I doubt that the apparent conflict can be entirely eliminated. To some extent, his asceticism probably is a deeply rooted mood or appetite, a temperamental disposition that is not utterly in conformity with all his explicit thoughts. But he is much more consistent, or closer to being consistent, than at first appears.

2. The Curse of Trade

In August 1837, Thoreau delivered an address at the commencement exercises for his class at Harvard on "The Commercial Spirit of Modern Times, Considered in Its Influence on the Political, Moral, and Literary Character of a Nation." The topic was assigned, but the sentiments he expressed were clearly his own:

> We are to look chiefly for the commercial spirit, and the power that still cherishes and sustains it, in a blind and unmanly love of wealth ... Let men, true to their natures, cultivate the moral affections, lead manly and independent lives; let them make riches the means and not the end of existence, and we will hear no more of the commercial spirit.[2]

The low value he places here on commerce and the result at which it aims—wealth—and the strong suggestion that morals and business are incompatible or nearly so are attitudes that he expressed throughout his career. As the years pass, they develop into a critique of trade that becomes far more subtle and nuanced, but they continue to give the impression of some sort of blanket condemnation. In *Walden*, the textual evidence ranges from numerous hostile asides, as when he comments that White Pond and Walden Pond "are too pure to have a market value; they contain no muck" (481.37–38), to at least one strikingly categorical statement: "Trade curses everything it handles; and though you trade in messages from heaven, the whole curse of trade attaches to the business" (378.2–4).

As I have already hinted, the reason I am discussing these ideas here is that they constitute another instance of asceticism, in precisely the same sense that applies to Thoreau's sometimes dim view of the physical appetites. I realize that this might strike some readers as odd thing to say. According to the informal understanding that many people have, the strictures of asceticism only extend to relatively brute animal appetites, to the pleasures of food, drink, and sex. But that is not what the word "asceticism" traditionally means, either in ethics or in theology.[3] Consider the fact that no religious order would be considered as practicing asceticism if it required a vow of chastity but not of poverty. Why not? The ascetic requirement of chastity is not an end in itself: it has a point. The point has something to do with the ascetic's attitude toward the deep consequences of the fact that human beings are *organisms*. The fact that human beings are entangled in physical nature, and tend to turn their attention and their desires toward it, impedes the realization of ideals that are prized by the ascetic. Ascetic requirements are meant to help us overcome such impediments, freeing us for pursuit of the ideal.

This entanglement of human attention and desire in physical nature is a consequence of the fact that human beings are not disembodied souls inhabiting a non-corporeal world but have needs and concerns that can only be satisfied by interacting in various ways with the physical environment. Inevitably, some of the physical effects they need or wish to bring about require them to use parts of nature other than their own bodies. The elements utilized may be either raw natural resources or objects made by human artifice from such resources and used as tools to bring about desired effects. Such objects and resources are what we call "wealth." Thus conceived, it becomes a truism that the acquisition of wealth uses up an enormous amount of the human being's time and attention. In a young and growing commercial society such as nineteenth-century America, it seems to exclude almost everything else.

An ascetic morality that contented itself with devaluing the pleasures of the flesh while ignoring the pursuit of wealth would be an irrational enterprise. It would have made an effort to counteract a few impediments to the achievement of its ideals while leaving another, very obvious and very powerful one unopposed. It seems fitting, then, that historically, ascetic codes take a dim view of wealth as well as of eating, drinking, and sex.

So far, Thoreau appears to fit the profile of the consistent and determined ascetic. Yet there is a problem. As with his views on eating and drinking, the problem is one of consistency. In chapter IV ("Sounds"), despite his many negative observations about commerce, he presents a surprisingly poetic, indeed Homeric, description of the train that races past Walden—"this traveling demigod, this cloud-compeller" (415.11–12)—and follows it immediately with a startling hymn to business. What is all the more startling since the praise in it is virtue-centered—it is based on traits of character that he attributes to commerce:

> What recommends commerce to me is its enterprise and bravery. It does not clasp its hands and pray to Jupiter. I see these men every day go about their business with more or less courage and content, doing more even than they suspect, and perchance better employed than they could have consciously devised... Commerce is unexpectedly confident and serene, alert, adventurous, and unwearied. It is very natural in its methods withal, far more so than many fantastic enterprises and sentimental experiments, and hence its singular success. (417.1–26)

There is an obvious difficulty in rendering this consistent with the author's attacks on commerce elsewhere, or indeed with his description (in the chapter "The Ponds") of the same train, just as Homeric in its way as the first one, but this time full of condemnation:

> That devilish Iron Horse, whose ear-rending neigh is heard throughout the town, has muddied the Boiling Spring with his foot, and he it is that has browsed off all the woods on Walden shore, that Trojan horse, with a thousand men in his belly, introduced by mercenary Greeks! (476.12–17)

I would like to overcome this difficulty—or at least a good part of it—by returning for the moment to the first of the two problems I have set out in this chapter: the difficulty of resolving the paradox of Thoreau's presenting himself as an ascetic worshipper of nature. The solution in both cases, I will argue, lies in understanding the peculiar nature of Thoreau's asceticism (IV.3 and IV.4). This will lead to an extended discussion (IV.5–9) of the nature of the anti-commercial side of his asceticism and an attempt to assess its coherence and plausibility.

3. Higher Laws and Lower

A key to understanding Thoreau's asceticism can be found at an important juncture in "Economy," where he has just made the declaration, which I discussed earlier (II.3), that the alternative to obtaining necessities is not to obtain superfluities "as more and richer food, larger and more splendid houses, finer and more abundant clothing, more numerous, incessant, and hotter fires, and the like" but to "adventure on life." He explains his preference for the "adventure" alternative: "The soil, it appears, is suited to the seed, for it has sent its radicle downward, and it may now send its shoot upward also with confidence. Why has man rooted himself thus firmly in the earth, but that he may rise in the same proportion into the heavens above?" (335.6–10). He is drawing an analogy here, in which the human being is compared to a seed planted in soil. The soil represents the comparatively worldly concerns of seeking food, clothing, and shelter, while the air above the soil indicates the higher concerns, which in comparison are non-worldly. He then elaborates on the analogy somewhat:

> for the nobler plants are valued for the fruit they bear at last in the air and light, far from the ground, and are not treated like the humbler esculents, which, though they may be biennials, are cultivated only till they have perfected their root, and often cut down at top for this purpose, so that most would not know them in their flowering season. (335.10–16)

Supposing that this analogy is in fact an analogical *argument*, it seems on its face to be quite implausible. In particular, the last-quoted part seems to be based on the quaint notion that we can distinguish between "nobler" and "humbler" plants.

However, I think the earlier part of this passage, the one in which the human being is explicitly likened to a seed, works rather differently and is more effective. It can also be seen as an analogical argument, but the assumptions that underlie it are more plausible. It might be spelled out along the following lines. He is claiming, implicitly, that in plant life, the functions that develop first are ones that serve to support the physical survival of the individual plant, though they derive their real importance from the fact that they support certain later-developing functions, which promote quite different results. He wants us to apply this same idea to human life: that the activities in which we interact with nature to support our survival are genuinely important but only because they support other functions which mature later and are of a fundamentally different nature. What serves to connect his premise about plant life with the conclusion about human life that he wishes to persuade us of is the unstated hypothesis that serves to *explain* why his comment about plant life is true. The reason why plant life has this character is that living organisms in general necessarily have the same character: all organisms survive by interacting with the physical world, but these functions derive their importance from the fact that they support other, very different ones, and they will accordingly be futile and pointless if these others are never carried out. (For more on the nature of analogical argument, see the "Appendix.")

Understood in this way, Thoreau's argument rests on the assumption that functions in nonhuman organisms can be related as means and end, so that the value that some functions have is derived from the fact that they support and facilitate the work done by others. It is also based on the distinct but closely related assumption that some functions have higher worth than others, an idea that we might call the idea of rank order among functions. To the extent that some activities only have value if they serve others, this would mean that they have a lower status than those others. These assumptions are obviously debatable, but they are (unlike the assumption that organisms themselves can be ranked by means of the seemingly ethical concepts of the noble and the humble) within the realm of the plausible. What is more immediately relevant to our present purposes is the considerable extent to which they can explain Thoreau's asceticism.

First, it might be helpful to take a step back to see the role that these notions play in Thoreau's scheme of values in general. To begin with one example, the notion of a rank order of functions underlies Thoreau's defense of reading in the third chapter of *Walden*. This defense, it must be said, is a somewhat unusual one in that it includes many attacks on the reading that people actually do and on the amount of time they spend doing it. Clearly, he makes a very big distinction of value between the things that people might read: whether one's reading has value depends to some extent on what one reads. He is eager to defend the classics of antiquity as most worth the time spent on them. However, there is an issue that is much more fundamental than that of what one reads, as he makes clear when he speaks of different ways of reading the ancient classics:

> They have only been read as the multitude read the stars, at most astrologically, not astronomically. Most men have learned to read to serve a paltry convenience, as they have learned to cipher in order to keep accounts and not be cheated in trade; but of reading as a noble intellectual exercise they know little or nothing; yet this only is reading, in a high sense, not that which lulls us as a luxury and suffers the nobler faculties to sleep the while, but what we have to stand on tip-toe to read and devote our most alert and wakeful hours to. (406.4–13)

To read astrologically would mean to read with a view to acquiring advice concerning one's concrete practical affairs, as opposed to reading with a view to grasping the nature of things, as we do when we study astronomy. What makes the higher sort of reading genuinely higher is not simply the worth of the truths it reveals to us but in addition the worth of the "nobler faculties" that are awakened as we contemplate these truths. It is these faculties that make reading a "noble" exercise.

In Thoreau's discussion of reading, the difference of value between different human activities is derived from a difference of value between the faculties employed in those activities. He sees the same sort of derivation in many other contexts. One instance can be found in his discussion of hunting and fishing in "Higher Laws." To some extent, that discussion is an attempt to devalue these activities on the grounds that they are not "agreeable to" his "imagination" (493.34–5). However, he also *defends* fishing in these same pages, and hunting as well, and in a distinctly Thoreauvian way:

> Fishermen, hunters, woodchoppers, and others, spending their lives in the fields and woods, in a peculiar sense a part of Nature themselves, are often in a more favorable mood for observing her, in the intervals of their pursuits, than philosophers or poets even, who approach her with expectation. She is not afraid to exhibit herself to them. (490.22–8)

The activities of hunting and fishing, even while we are doing them, can develop a faculty that Thoreau prizes highly: the attentive observation of nature. He sees such faculties as playing a similar sort of role in human development, so that the initially petty and less-than-noble activity of pursuing and killing wild animals can lead to loftier things in the future. When parents ask him whether they should allow their children to hunt, he answers, "Yes, ... *make* them hunters, though sportsmen only at first, if possible, mighty hunters at last, so that they shall not find game large enough for them in this or any vegetable wilderness-hunters as well as fishers of men" (491.35–9).

Thoreau's seeming vacillation between attacking these activities and defending them makes perfect sense if we interpret his comments in light of the rank order of functions. On this interpretation, the problem with hunting and fishing is not that they are positively immoral. It lies in the fact that, as ordinarily done, they carry out relatively low-level functions. But they can also serve as means to loftier ones. For Thoreau, this fact fully redeems them. If they support or facilitate some higher function, then they are productive of something of great value, and that would make *them* very valuable as well. The same activity can have both high value and low value, depending on how it is done.

It is obvious that hunting and fishing are not uniquely special cases here: Thoreau is committed to some general principle concerning the relations that generally hold between the higher and lower, the nobler and baser functions and capacities. If what he is saying of these activities is true, then the same would have to be true of other relevantly similar aspects of human life. The principle involved would seem to be this: that, if some lower capacity or function comes to support or facilitate something higher, then, so long as this remains true, it is good and not bad.

This principle leads logically to a position that is clearly ascetic, provided that we add two more premises. Both are, if not obviously true, then at least plausible and defensible. The first, in fact, is really a corollary of the principle itself. If it is true that lower things that support higher ones thereby become good, then another idea would seem with equal force to be true: namely, that lower things that interfere with higher ones thereby become, in that context, not merely lower but *positively bad*. This is the first premise. The second is the notion that a certain class of human functions, namely those that are most intimately connected with the physical basis of human life, are lower than certain other functions and, furthermore, have a natural tendency to interfere with or displace those higher ones when they do not positively support them.

I suggest that Thoreau does accept these assumptions more or less consistently and that this suggestion will go far in neutralizing the paradoxical appearance of his asceticism. First, and most obviously, it holds the promise of explaining why he tends to make remarks that appear to be generally hostile toward the activities by which human beings support their continued survival. Such remarks would be natural enough if he thinks that such activities have a certain tendency to interfere with others that are by nature higher than they are.

More importantly, though perhaps equally obviously, the same suggestion can help to explain why his hostility toward these functions is not persistent but rather coexists with attitudes that seem to view them favorably. The sort of asceticism I attribute to him is of a rather distinctive sort. It is very different from the sort that would characterize an ethic of religious dualism, in which objects are sorted forever into sharply sundered categories of good and evil. The grosser functions of the human organism, in his view, are not bad in themselves but *become* bad when they enter into certain relations with the rest of the individual's life.[4] When these relations do not hold, the grosser function might in that case be positively good. In the latter case, a favorable attitude toward them would be entirely appropriate. We have already collected some information about what these relations are, but it would be well to pause now to sort out what we have seen, in preparation for extending it further and in new directions.

4. How Good Things Become Bad

One relation that can make such activities bad is the fact that they spring from certain sources in the soul of the agent, from certain states of mind. As we saw in Thoreau's discussion of reading, activities become noble or base as they spring from nobler or baser "faculties." He applies this principle to the activity of eating as well. "A puritan may go to his brown-bread crust with as gross an appetite as ever an alderman to his turtle. Not that food which entereth into the mouth defileth a man, but the appetite with which it is eaten" (496.25–8).

Why would the appetite that drives an activity have this sort of decisive importance? The most general answer, suggested by what we have already seen, is that the appetite is what prevents the act from having the right relation with the rest of life. He tells us that what defiles is "neither the quality nor the quantity, but the devotion to sensual savors; when that which is eaten is not a viand to sustain our animal, or inspire our spiritual life, but food for the worms that possess us" (496.28–32). In this case, the state of mind from which the activity springs is harmful because it is a state of "devotion" and because this devotion is directed toward "sensual savors."

Why would it be so harmful to act on devotion of this sort? Thoreau does not produce a detailed answer to this question, but neither does he leave us entirely in the dark:

> "The soul not being mistress of herself," says Thseng-tseu, "one looks, and one does not see; one listens, and one does not hear; one eats, and one does not know the savor of food." He who distinguishes the true savor of his food can never be a glutton; he who does not cannot be otherwise. (496.20–5)

The idea that underlies this comment is similar to one that Aristotle uses in his discussion of temperance in the *Nicomachean Ethics*. Aristotle's notion appears when he is expressing his view, which seems rather curious at first, that gluttons are not really concerned with savors at all: "But even taste appears to play but a small part, if any, in temperance. For taste is concerned with discriminating flavors, as is done by wine-tasters, and cooks preparing savory dishes."[5] Aristotle believes that gluttons are really most interested in the physical act of eating and with the tactile sensations associated with engulfing portions of the world, an attitude he symbolizes with an anecdote about a gourmand who wished he had a neck as long as a crane's, so as to prolong the experience of swallowing.[6]

The idea that underlies both Aristotle's comments and Thoreau's would seem to involve some very close connection between virtue and consciousness. The connection is sufficiently close to indicate that a trait that involves distinguishing the true flavors of food cannot be gluttony. Such a trait is too closely akin to virtue. In Aristotle, this idea is closely allied to his idea of *theoria*—approximately translatable as contemplation—as the highest state that human beings can attain and to the idea of virtue as something that both supports and to some extent shares in this state. In Thoreau, there is a fundamentally important idea that is in fact relevantly similar to *theoria*.

When this idea appears in *Walden* it is often described as the state of *wakefulness*.[7] Thoreau associates wakefulness with images of dawn and morning and he often uses them to represent it ("morning is when I am awake and there is a dawn in me" [394.1–2]). Perhaps the most memorable instance of this is to be found in the last two sentences of the book: "There is more day to dawn. The sun is but a morning star." Just as conspicuous, if not quite as memorable, is the epigraph that appears on the title page, in which he proposes "to brag as lustily as chanticleer in the morning, standing on his roost, if only to wake my neighbors up." Indeed, if we consider the epigraph (which is not a quotation from another author but a sentence from the text itself) to be the beginning of *Walden*, we can say that it is like "Civil Disobedience" in that it begins where it ends: in this case, with intimations of awakening. In both works, this symmetry serves to emphasize the themes that appear at both their termini. In *Walden*, of course, there are many explicit statements of the theme thus emphasized, such as "moral reform is the effort to throw off sleep" (394.2–3), "we must learn to reawaken and keep ourselves awake" (394.13), and this one, which comes near to attributing divinity to the person who is wide awake:

> The millions are awake enough for physical labor; but only one in a million is awake enough for effective intellectual exertion, only one in a hundred millions to a poetic or divine life. To be awake is to be alive. I have never yet met a man who was quite awake. How could I have looked him in the face? (394.7–12)

Perhaps Thoreau is thinking of passages in the Bible in which God reveals Himself to humans only indirectly, by means of images such as a burning bush, as if direct revelation would be impossible to behold, and even then the sight is typically too terrifying for the one who receives the revelation. "And Moses hid his face; for he was afraid to look upon God."

The human seed has sent its radicle downward in order to approach this sort of consciousness. That is the point. On this view, attentive awareness is intrinsically good, presumably even including awareness of the flavors of foods. The ideal of wakefulness thus helps to resolve the apparent contradiction in Thoreau's thinking, that of the ascetic nature-worshipper. It reveals complexity where it had seemed there was only contradiction. Whether a trait that seeks worldly goods is a vice or not depends not on the worldly thing itself but on the relationship between the trait and this ideal. In a certain way, his thinking is hierarchical: a thing is good if it plays its proper role in the hierarchy, and bad if it plays some role contrary to it.

This same ideal also complicates Thoreau's scheme of values in another way. In contrasting those who are awake enough for physical labor with those who are more fully awake, he is making a judgment in which he makes some sort of distinction of value among the lives of human beings in general. He is saying that wakefulness is a superior good, and that it is such for everyone. His thinking on this subject is not only hierarchical but universal as well. If the millions were awake enough for effective intellectual exertion, they would be living better lives. This, for better or worse, is the one exception he makes to the pluralistic vitalism I described in the earlier. The standard of value here is not the individual genius of the agent about whom the judgment is being made. One good is placed above others, and for everyone.

Thoreau's universalism, as it might be called, may or may not be entirely consistent with the pluralism I attributed to him earlier. I will have a little more to say about that later; for the moment, it is well to notice that these ideas both arise from the same basic Thoreauvian principle: namely, his vitalism. Being awake is so important to him because, as he has just said, "to be awake is to be alive." He does not spell this idea out in detail and there are, of course, many questions that he leaves open. He does not discuss, for instance, whether he means it to apply to all animate beings or only to human beings. But one thing is clear: he believes that, at least for human beings, to live is to be conscious. When he says that he went to Walden because he "wanted to live deep and suck out all the marrow of life" to "drive life into a corner, and reduce it to its lowest terms, and, if it proved to be mean, why then to get the whole and genuine meanness of it, and publish its meanness to the world" (394.33-9), he means to say something that is more or less literally true: he was seeking life. He could have worked in John Thoreau's pencil business—as indeed he had done and would do again—but he would have been less conscious than he was when he was living in the woods, and he would consequently have been less alive.[8]

5. Exchange-Avoidance

Perhaps for reasons of Victorian delicacy, Thoreau's discussion of the urges connected with food, drink, and sex contain no detailed account of the ways in which they are related, for good or ill, to the highest functions of human life. As we have seen, he does indicate that both sorts of relations, both positive and negative, do exist, but he says little about what they are. In the case of commerce he suffers from no such delicacy, and a significant portion of *Walden* is devoted to analysis and critique of economic matters and their relations to the wider context of human life.

As I have suggested, the project he recounts in *Walden*—the project the recounting of which gives the book its narrative structure—is an attempt to solve the economic problem with which his peculiar genius confronts him. He illuminates his own problem by describing an analogous problem faced by an American Indian who visited Concord: "Not long since, a strolling Indian went to sell baskets at the house of a well-known lawyer in my neighborhood. 'Do you wish to buy any baskets?' he asked. 'No, we do not want any,' was the reply. 'What!' exclaimed the Indian as he went out the gate, 'do you mean to starve us?'" (337.28–32).

Henry speculates that the unfortunate Indian must have noticed "that the lawyer had only to weave arguments, and, by some magic, wealth and standing followed," and reasoned something like this: "I will go into business; I will weave baskets; it is a thing which I can do. Thinking that when he had made the baskets he would have done his part, and then it would be the white man's to buy them" (337.35–8). The Indian's mistake is failing to realize that making the baskets was not nearly enough; it was also "necessary for him to make it worth the other's while to buy them, or at least make him think that it was so, or to make something else which it would be worth his while to buy" (337.35–338.2).[9]

His own situation, he says, is like that of the Indian: "I too had woven a kind of basket of a delicate texture"—probably referring to the disastrous publication of *A Week on the Concord and Merrimack Rivers*—but, he says, "I had not made it worth any one's while to buy them." Thoreau and the Indian visitor are like the lawyer in that both have woven, have produced something. They are unlike him, though, in that they have not chosen to make this particular product because others already want it, nor have they altered the desires of others to make them fit the products that they independently wished to make. They are also alike in that both are inclined to weave their baskets anyway. Yet, unlike the Indian, who seems to insist that people buy his baskets despite their own desires, Thoreau chooses rather to investigate "how to avoid the necessity of selling them" (338.2–7).

The Indian and the lawyer represent two opposite reactions to commercial society. The lawyer, following the promptings of the market, generates a product for the purpose of selling it. The Indian wishes to supplant such a commercial exchange with a noncommercial exchange, in which money is given to him not out of a desire to own one of his baskets but out of other motives, such as compassion or guilt. The giving of money would in that case not be a pure purchase but, to some extent, a *gift*. Thoreau's alternative to both these reactions to commerce is radically to reduce the amount of time he must spend on activities aimed at producing something marketable. The result will be, to a certain extent, to avoid exchange altogether.

It will help in understanding the nature of Thoreau's alternative to realize, first, that the Indian's position is not nearly as impractical as he makes it sound. It does represent a genuine option, alternative to both Thoreau's position and the lawyer's. The native basket maker comes from a culture in which, at least until recently, the exchanges by which people had acquired the wherewithal to live often really were, very often, exchanges of gifts. In such a context, to say, "What! Do you mean to starve us?" to someone who refuses to make a gift could actually make perfect sense. Gifts, in particular, gifts of food, were obligatory by custom and a crucial means of survival.[10]

Admittedly, the system of gift exchange was not in effect in white America, then or now, and for all I know it may already have been in a state of decay in the tribe of Concord's Indian visitor. But in our world it is still possible to get along by noncommercial exchanges that are similar in certain ways to the one in which he wishes to engage. Acting in concert with other basket makers, one could force others to pay for one's baskets despite the fact that they do not desire to own them, perhaps by getting a government subsidy for the preservation of native arts. Again, one might forcibly eliminate the consumer's alternatives to taking one's baskets, perhaps by having the government impose burdensome taxes or crippling regulations on the manufacturers of non-basket containers. I mention these possibilities because, although Thoreau is plainly not thinking of them here as genuine options, they are relevant to the logic of his own position. Such strategies force certain noncommercial exchange relations on everyone and so tend to make the market unavailable to those who genuinely desire it. They would replace the commercial system of relations with what you might call, if it were not a contradiction, a *forced gift* system. It is an important feature of Thoreau's alternative that it does not have this effect. It does not take commercial exchange away from those who prefer it.

6. Thoreauvian Economy

Stanley Cavell has pointed out that "Economy," the first chapter of *Walden* and the one that "establishes the underlying vocabulary of the book as a whole," contains a remarkable variety of terms having to do with economic matters:

> There is profit and loss, rich and poor, cost and expense, borrow and pay, owe and own, business, commerce, enterprises, ventures, affairs, capital, price, amount, improvement, bargain, employment, inheritance, bankruptcy, work, trade, labor, idle, spend, waste, allowance, fortune, gain, earn, afford, possession, change, settling, living, interest, prospects, means, terms.[11]

This is not surprising, since a large part of Thoreau's purpose, in this chapter and in the rest of the book, is to express and justify his view of commercial concerns. What *is* surprising, given that this view seems to be largely critical, is the fact that he uses this language to characterize his *own* project: "I have always endeavored to acquire strict business habits; they are indispensable to every man" (338.23-4).

Perhaps the most complex of all these economic words is the title of the first chapter itself: economy. To some extent, the meaning Thoreau attaches to this word antedates the theories of modern economists: in antiquity, "economy" (*oikonomika*) referred to the art of stewardship or household management, and to the order or plan of the world as a whole. Certainly Thoreau, who calls our attention to the minutiae of his own household, and at the same time to the largest possible view of the context in which we all act, would claim that he pays close attention to economy in both these senses. Also applicable to *Walden* is the sense in which "economy" is contrasted with waste, as in "her performance showed a great economy of means." For waste is one of his principal accusations against his world and its opposite is one of his own cherished standards of value. It seems on the face of it that the only familiar sense of the word that does *not* apply to the ideas in this book is the most obvious one, in which it refers to the body of theory that deals with cost, profit, loss, and related ideas, and which was used (or misused) in his time to justify an exclusive concern with pecuniary matters. Nonetheless, a closer look shows that he appropriates precisely these sorts of ideas and, suitably changed, makes them his own. The act of appropriation is part of a clever attempt to show that economic theories as commonly used are actually *un*economical in virtually every sense of the word.[12]

He makes this vocabulary his own, in the first place, by taking a single very basic economic term and giving it a Thoreauvian meaning. The particular word he chooses reflects a judgment that some academic economists would also make: that the idea of *cost* is the fundamental concept in any truly economic way of thinking.[13] The "cost of a thing," he says, "is the amount of what I will call life which is required to be exchanged for it, immediately or in the long run" (347.17–19). If this is what cost is, then the *benefit* of the thing would seem to be how much of what the author calls life would be produced or saved by it. Once this determination has been made, it is a relatively simple matter to produce a Thoreauvian conception of profit: in his terms, profit would be the extent to which benefit exceeds cost, in the event that benefit does exceed cost. It will be the *net* life-enhancing effects of the thing. Loss, by the same sort of reasoning, would be the extent to which the opposite relationship holds between cost and benefit, in the event that it does.

Having come this far, one is in a position to either define or qualify the significance of virtually all the terms in Cavell's impressive list. Obviously, we will have wandered into a world that is quite different from that of standard economics. The root of the difference lies in the fact that, in effect, Thoreau has done something that an economist cannot do, without ceasing to be an economist: he has specified, quite generally, what the maximand, the good that is to be maximized, is to be. It is life. For various reasons, economists do not do this. What is being maximized in the calculations of the economist is simply *value*, and value generally means something more or less equivalent to *whatever it is that people want*.

If one takes value (in this sense, as whatever people want) as one's maximand, one's ability to view one's economic system critically is limited. It will ordinarily make no sense to ask, for instance, whether a house is "really" worth its market price. Provided only that they knew what the house is like and how much money they were paying for it, the uncoerced choices of buyers have already told us all there is to know about such an issue. It must have been worth it to them, and what it is worth to them is the end of the matter, necessarily.

Once Thoreau specifies the maximand as he has, however, that is not the end of the matter for him. Part of the reason is suggested by the fact that he describes his standard of value as "what I will call life." "What I will call ... " is a locution by which scholars signal their readers that they are introducing a bit of technical terminology. Thoreau is warning us that he is using a specific conception of what life is, one that may not be ours, at least not until he has had a chance to convey it to us. Further, even if we do share his conception of what life is, we may not be striving to maximize it. If we do share his conception of the maximand, this brings other commitments with it: from within the point of view defined by his standard, it makes perfect sense to ask whether a house is worth what any one person, or any group of people, is willing to pay for it. It even makes sense to ask whether commercial society itself is worth what it costs.

7. Critique of Commerce

However, asking such a question is a very different matter from getting any particular answer: asking whether a house is worth what people are usually willing to pay is not the same thing as showing that it generally is not. In order to show that it is not, and in order more generally to cast doubt on the value of commercial society as we know it, Thoreau will need to assess the true cost, the *vital* cost, of a social arrangement that economists have long recognized as essential to commercial society.

Early in *The Wealth of Nations*, Adam Smith describes this social arrangement and succinctly explains its importance:

> When the division of labor has been once thoroughly established, it is but a very small part of a man's wants which the produce of his own labor can supply. He supplies the far greater part of them by exchanging that surplus part of his own labor, which is over and above his own consumption, for such parts of the produce of other men's labor as he has occasion for. Every man thus lives by exchanging, or becomes in some measure a merchant, and the society itself grows to be what is properly a commercial society.[14]

As Smith suggests, the division of labor more or less inevitably brings with it a heavy reliance on commerce. To the extent that one's productive efforts are specialized, one must get things that one desires from others, or not get them at all. Since the ways of getting things from others that are alternative to trade (which include begging as well as more coercive methods, such as theft) are not considered as options for normal adults, the inevitable result follows: one becomes a trader. For more or less that same reason, the reverse relationship also holds: As reliance on trade increases, so specialization must also increase. Traders are specialists, and those who specialize must trade.

If there is something bad about the division of labor as such, then the same consideration counts, in full, as a fault of commerce as well. It is precisely on this point that Thoreau focuses his critique of commerce. In very large part, his critique of commerce is a critique of the division of labor:

> What does architecture amount to in the experience of the mass of men? I never in all my walks came across a man engaged in so simple and natural an occupation as building his house. We belong to the community. It is not the tailor alone who is the ninth part of a man; it is as much the preacher, and the merchant, and the farmer. Where is this division of labor to end? and what object does it finally serve? No doubt another may also think for me; but it is

not therefore desirable that he should do so to the exclusion of my thinking for myself. (359.9-18)

Actually, there are two objections here to the division of labor. One of them is in a way more fundamental. The other could be seen as a rebuttal to a defense that might be offered in behalf of the division of labor.

The more fundamental objection flows naturally out of the conception of human life we examined earlier, in which life is viewed as a certain process in which individuals follow the promptings of their inner selves. The notion of the inner self as an originating source of action, one's genius as Thoreau often calls it, is obviously crucial to the position he is taking here. The ideal he is now setting up seems to be that of becoming the complete human being one has it in oneself to be. Yet the relationship that holds between individuals and their own identity is characterized by an odd sort of complexity: he describes my identity as *affected by* my behavior and, in particular, by the fact that I do or do not follow the promptings of my inner self. If I only follow the promptings of part of myself—say the part that is realized or satisfied by the activities of tailoring—and suppress or ignore all the rest, then the rest of my identity is somehow obliterated. I am only "part of a man." Though this inner nature is one's real self, it is not complete, or does not exist fully, unless it is realized in action.

Though I have stated them rather paradoxically, there is an obvious intuitive appeal to these ideas. While my true self does seem to be something "inner," it also seems true that these inner possibilities, if not acted on, remain *mere* possibilities. If it is good to exist and live, then there is always something regrettable about the fact that I did not pursue some activity of which I am capable. Some part of life and existence is denied me, some part that could have been mine. The greatest extreme to which this sort of loss can be carried would occur if I were to let another think for me "to the exclusion of my thinking for myself." The result would be the extinction of an individual human self. No matter what the benefits, Thoreau believes, such a thing cannot be worth it: "It costs more than it comes to" (368.28).

Here some people would surely point out the collective benefits of the division of labor. Though it may mean a constriction of individual vitality, this is merely, as Thoreau suggests, a cost. We can only know whether the cost of a thing is an objection to it if we first compare it to the benefits it brings with it. In this case, the loss to the individual, if that is what it is, brings with it an incalculable development of the economic system as a whole. Subsistence farmers, who consume only their own product, are like soloists, while people who practice the division of labor are like members of an orchestra. As members of the group, we can produce something that we cannot hope to achieve alone.

Thoreau's response to this argument would of course not be based on the idea that the defender of the division of labor should not try to find benefits that offset its costs. He implicitly recognizes the possibility of this sort of defensive move when he speaks of the relevant social arrangements as costing more than they come to: he is agreeing that they do come to something and that what they do come to is relevant to their total worth. As to what his response would most likely be, some notion of its general direction can be gathered from his brief comment that under a division of labor "we belong to the community." Insofar as this defense of the division of labor is founded on the value that these arrangements have for the group, for the social system of which the individual is a part, he would claim that the benefits are located in the wrong place. If that is all that can be said for them, if the division of labor is really a matter of the individual losing some quantum of vitality, which is then transferred to the group, then it would surely be a great evil. It would simply be one more master-slave relationship, of which the oppressed subject is the individual and the oppressive owner the community. "We belong to the community," he says. To the oppressed individual in this relationship he would no doubt apply the same principle that he applies to the ancient Egyptians who built the pyramids: "As for the Pyramids, there is nothing to wonder at in them so much as the fact that so many men could be found degraded enough to spend their lives constructing a tomb for some ambitious booby, whom it would have been wiser and manlier to have drowned in the Nile, and then given his body to the dogs" (368.18–24). If the value of the division of labor is that it somehow adds to the glory of the master that the individual serves, then, even if this master is a collectivity to which the individual belongs, this fact cannot justify its diminishing the life of the individual.

One gets the impression, from the generally individualistic tenor of Thoreau's writings, that one of the assumptions that undergirds this line of reasoning is something like this: quite aside from the fact that the collectivity is no more entitled to exploit individuals than a Pharaoh would be, it suffers from additional deficiency: it, unlike the Pharaoh, does not exist. Under this assumption, to transfer value from the individual to the collective is to take it away from something and give it to nothing. But there is another assumption at work here as well, one that is probably more important to him and is certainly more explicitly and emphatically presented in the pages of "Economy." He would claim that, in addition to the fact that this defense of the division of labor locates the benefits of a division of labor in the wrong place, it also picks out the wrong *sort* of benefit. The cost of the division of labor is a very important one, as he understands it: the good that we thereby lose is very closely related to that self-development in response to the promptings of one's own genius, which, as we saw earlier, he treats as identical to virtue. The value he attaches to this sort of self-development is distinctly ethical in nature. On the other hand, the vast structural complexity that the division of labor makes possible in the communities that are founded upon it does not seem to be an ethical characteristic at all.

In effect, Henry is challenging us to find a benefit that really would justify a loss of ethical value. Clearly he would say that this challenge is not met by the response we have just considered, because it makes the ethically objectionable move of sacrificing the individual to the community. He would also say that it is not met by the sort of response that is most commonly given by economists on the ground that it is not an ethical response at all. Adam Smith and many of his colleagues have pointed out what Smith called the "great increase of the quantity of work which, in consequence of the division of labor, the same number of people are capable of performing."[15] Much of *Walden* is dedicated to reminding us that material gains cannot offset losses of vitality and virtue. One cannot justify a loss of ethical value by claiming that one was paid—literally paid—for losing it. If the thing lost is ethical in nature, then such payments are simply temptations, and temptations must be resisted. To find a value that *would* justify the losses involved is the challenge Thoreau throws at his readers.

8. Another Response to Thoreau's Challenge

I will spend the next two sections commenting on whether this challenge can be met and, more generally, trying to evaluate Thoreau's ascetic arguments in general. In a way, the issue presented by his critique of the division of labor is a simple one. His line of reasoning consists in an attempt to substantiate two claims: first, that the division of labor has a certain effect on human life and, second, that this effect constitutes a cost and a heavy one. Accordingly, one's critical response could be to attack either the first claim or the second: one could try to show either that the division of labor does not have the effects he claims it has, or that they are not too costly.

One way of making such a response would probably seem obvious to many people. Despite its relative obviousness, I think it is misconceived. It is worth discussing, though, because it will give us a chance to look more closely at what

Thoreau is actually saying. The objection I have in mind can be stated in various different ways. Here is one of them.

Essentially, the effect that Thoreau finds the division of labor has on human life is that it prevents us from doing everything that in some sense we could have done. That is, the standard of excellence against which he measures it, his ideal, is to develop all sides of one's personality. But this standard is *arbitrarily* stringent and would lead to nihilistic consequences. The simple fact of the matter is that in order to accomplish one thing you must, at least for the moment, give up indefinitely many other things that you might have done. Of course, the fact that one *cannot* do everything simultaneously does not prevent one from doing things seriatim: having given up other things to do in order to do one, I can still do some of those other things later, after I have done the one. However, I will not live forever, and I can never come close to doing all the things that I might have done. The nature of reality is such that one cannot develop all sides of one's individuality. Thoreau's objection to the division of labor, that it does not allow us to develop all sides of ourselves but rather requires us to cut ourselves off from parts of what we might have been, could also be raised against reality itself.

This objection attributes to Thoreau a standard that he himself does not explicitly state. His comments do seem to commit him to the idea that the fact that something prevents one from developing some aspect of one's individuality constitutes a cost that the thing brings with it. Do they also commit him to the view that the ideal, what we really should be doing if we can, is to develop all sides ourselves, doing everything that we have it in ourselves to do? There is a simple reason for hoping that they do not commit him to this, at least if we desire his position to be consistent with itself. For this ideal conflicts with a Thoreauvian standard I have already discussed at length: the notion that an individual should follow his or her own genius. For one's genius is something that prompts us to do particular things, things that are presumably different from other things that one could have done. To follow it is actually incompatible with doing everything that one can do.

I maintain that Thoreau's comments do not commit him to holding both of these mutually contradictory standards. Indeed, it is impossible to understand the logic of the things he says unless we realize that he does not contradict himself in this way. It is a very important fact about the concept of cost that it does not commit one to the view that costs should never be incurred. It does not mean that the ideal, or what we should be doing, is to avoid incurring any costs. This in fact constitutes part of the difference between, on the one hand, seeing something as a cost and, on the other, seeing it as a violation of a duty. Cost is that which we *should* incur, so long as it is worth it, but no further. A violation of duty, in contrast, is simply that which we should not do: a question of how much we should do it or how far we should pursue it does not even arise. With violations of duty, the inference that this objection seems to attribute to Thoreau makes perfect sense: If *a*, *b*, and *c* are violations of duty, then the ideal, what we should be doing, includes (at minimum) the nonoccurrence of *a*, *b*, and *c*. The optimal course of action will always be one in which such things are not done. With costs, however, this last claim is not true. For any given cost, it may well be that we should incur it. Consequently, if failure to develop any one aspect of one's personality is merely a cost, then it does not follow that developing every aspect is what we should be doing.

The question of course, as far as the interpretation of Thoreau is concerned, is whether he recognizes this. Does he speak of the division of labor in a way that indicates that he recognizes that it should be pursued up to a point, that the issue is not whether we do it at all but how far we take it? Yes, he certainly does. Consider his defense of his interesting claim that, in the founding of a college the buildings should be built, at least to a significant extent, by the students themselves. Concerning the alternative and more usual arrangement, he has this to say:

> The mode of founding a college is, commonly, to get up a subscription of dollars and cents, and then, following blindly the principles of a division of labor to its extreme—a principle which should never be followed but with circumspection—to call in a contractor who makes this a subject of speculation, and he employs Irishmen or other operatives actually to lay the foundations, while the students that are to be are said to be fitting themselves for it; and for these oversights successive generations have to pay. (362.25–33)

He is criticizing this mode of founding a college, oddly enough, for its *lack* of economy. Those effects for which future generations will "have to pay" are hidden and deferred costs, which this method has failed to minimize. The costs in question are imposed by its use of the division of labor, in which the quotidian work of the college is done by poor Irish workers, while the students (theoretically) do nothing but learn.

To convince us that the costs in this case are too high, he asks us to consider the approaches applied to the study of metallurgy:

> Which would have advanced the most at the end of a month—the boy who had made his own jackknife from the ore which he had dug and smelted, reading as much as would be necessary for this—or the boy who had attended the

lectures on metallurgy at the Institute in the meanwhile, and had received a Rogers penknife from his father? Which would be most likely to cut his fingers? (363.20–6)

By pursuing the principle of the division of labor too far, the institution fails to maximize its maximand. Ultimately, of course, this goal is life, but in the case of an educational institution the immediate goal is the production of knowledge, or of knowledge vitalistically conceived, as intelligence that enables one to live one's life.

The alternative to the more usual approach would not be to abandon the division of labor altogether. Obviously, the program of having the students do the labor of the college, if it were pushed too far, could easily interfere with rather than promote their education. If the students were to try to do all the jobs needed to keep the college running, that could result in their spending all their time in physical labor, which would likely mean that they are no longer "reading as much as would be necessary" for learning something from their hands-on activities. The plausible alternative to the approach Thoreau is criticizing is to pursue the division of labor as long as it promotes the end, which of course is education, and then stop. Thoreau says as much, though he puts it negatively, when he comments that the principle of the division of labor is a principle that "should never be followed but with circumspection." By making our want of circumspection (that is, looking all around, or taking every relevant factor into account) his objection, he implies that, if the principle really is followed *with* circumspection, he can have no objection to it. He is discussing the possibility of following it without circumspection because he wishes to warn us against our powerful tendency, as he sees it, to take the principle too far. That there is also such a thing as following it far enough is something that we have no need to hear. However, the notion that such a thing as far enough does exist is both consistent with everything he says and, in fact, implicit in it.

Read in this light, the two questions I have already quoted are not rhetorical ones: "Where is this division of labor to end? and what object does it finally serve?" (359.15–16). Where the principle should end is indeed the question. Further, the answer to the second question yields the answer to the first. If we know the end it is to serve, we have at least the basis for knowledge of where it should end. If Thoreau's idea were that the division of labor should never begin, that we really should develop all sides of our natures, then his doctrine would be simpler, but at the same time less coherent, than it is.

9. Relevant Benefits of Commerce

Thoreau's thinking on these issues literally is an instance of "economy," in the same sense of the word in which it applies to the thinking of the economist: he is single-mindedly concerned with profit and loss, with the maximization of value and the avoidance of waste. His charge—which is no mere rhetorical trick—is that the use of economic theories that pays heed only to pecuniary values is actually profoundly uneconomical. In a certain way, his critique overlaps certain theoretical advances made by economists themselves since his day, in which the concept of cost was expanded to include opportunity cost in general.[16] According to this way of thinking, the cost of a good is the most highly valued thing—whether its value is pecuniary or not—that must be forgone in order to achieve that good. You could say that revising cost as opportunity cost is just what Thoreau is attempting to do here.

Before making a final attempt to say something about the cogency of his critique of commerce, it would be helpful to pause and take stock of his argument as we have seen it, to see just how radical the critique is, how much there is for us to agree or disagree with. The very fact that he means his charge literally enhances its rhetorical power, but it also has the effect of placing certain limits on what he is able to say. It requires him to use, and use correctly, the concept of cost, and this concept too brings certain constraints with it. He does identify his maximand and, as we have seen, this fact actually removes some of the constraints under which the economist labors: unlike the economist, he need not accept whatever people desire as values. However, this liberating effect is only partial. The reason for this we have already seen. Life for Thoreau means following one's own genius. While one's genius is not the same thing as one's desires (it is not necessarily identical to any of one's desires, much less to all of them taken together), it does have one thing in common with personal desires: it differs from one person to the next. Thus, although his method does not compel him to accept all the wants that each individual has as standards of value, he does have to accept the vagaries of individual genius.

This is a potentially serious constraint. As we have seen (II.6), it compels him to state that his devaluation of philanthropy does not apply to everyone. By the same sort of reasoning, it would also seem that his criticisms of commerce will not apply to everyone either. If people really are very different from one another, it seems likely there will be people whose geniuses will indeed be served by specializing their efforts and selling their product on the market. As a matter of fact, Thoreau is consistent enough to say this, and with considerable emphasis. In the midst of his critique of commerce in "Economy," he issues a disclaimer to the effect that he does not "mean to prescribe rules to strong and valiant natures" who "build more magnificently and spend more lavishly than the richest, without ever impoverishing themselves" nor to "those who find their encouragement and inspiration in precisely the present condition of things, and cherish it with the fondness and enthusiasm of lovers." Neither does he mean to prescribe to "those who are well employed, in whatever circumstances" (335.17–28). To a significant extent, the reason Thoreau finds that he must minimize his own participation in the market is that he faces a problem analogous to that of the Indian basket maker. The problem is that the activity to which his genius leads him has little or no market value: few people will voluntarily pay him to do it. This problem will not be faced by those who find that their vitally rewarding activities do have market value.

Though it will still be true that, by specializing and narrowing their range of activities, such people will be cutting themselves off from large portions of what they might have been, and this fact will count as a cost of sorts, this is no more true of them than it is of all those who cut back their participation in commercial society in order to follow their genius. In the latter case, the benefits of this, for Thoreau, are worth these costs. Even in his "experiment" at Walden, Thoreau does not rigidly apply the notion of exchange-avoidance to himself. His work in the bean field, the subject of the seventh chapter of his book, is far from being a case of subsistence farming. As he tells us, "I am by nature a Pythagorean, so far as beans are concerned [i.e., like Pythagoras, he does not eat them] ... , and exchanged them for rice" (451.26–8). The bean rows were a strictly commercial enterprise; he raised them to sell them and purchase something he wanted more. He became for the season something of a specialist in bean production, thus pursuing the division of labor (but with circumspection).

His main criticism of commerce and the division of labor—that it can be too costly in terms of self-development and the following of one's genius—is one he admits does not apply to everyone. Nonetheless, despite its less-than-universal scope, it is clear he thinks this criticism is a serious one. Immediately after he tells us that he does not mean to prescribe to valiant natures, he says that *Walden* is addressed instead "mainly to the mass of men who are discontented, and idly complaining of the hardness of their lot or of the times" (335.28–29). Plainly, by "mass of men" he means to refer to an enormous number of people, probably in fact to most people. Most of us would be better off significantly reducing our involvement in the commercial nexus, and finding alternative ways to get along, perhaps for the most part by the simple expedient of getting along on less. We have overinvested our lives in it. Its returns do not justify the amount of life we have spent on it. This is what his critique of commercial society comes to.

This critique is less extreme than other, more familiar criticisms of commerce, but it nonetheless represents a serious charge concerning the human value of trade. The only way to answer this charge effectively would be to find reason to believe that the costs are less or that the relevant benefits are greater than he supposes.

Do we have any good reason to believe either of these things? I would like to suggest that we do. One of them is a quite general reason to doubt that the costs of commerce are as great as he thinks they are. The other takes the form of a considerable benefit, one that Thoreau himself arguably should recognize as an ethical benefit and therefore very relevant to the issue at hand.

The first of these reasons to resist Thoreau's critique of commerce is an objection that is often raised against a certain sort of individualism, sometimes justly and sometimes not. One of the unjust instances, I believe, is a criticism that John Gray makes of a certain central argument of John Stuart Mill's *On Liberty*, in which Mill borrows a theme from a remarkable book by Wilhelm von Humboldt.[17] This is what Mill says:

> Few persons, out of Germany, even comprehend the meaning of the doctrine which Wilhelm von Humboldt made the text of a treatise—that "the end of man, or that which is prescribed by the eternal or immutable dictates of reason, and not suggested by vague and transient desires, is the highest and most harmonious development of his powers to a complete and consistent whole;" that, therefore, the object "towards which every human being must ceaselessly direct his efforts, and on which especially those who design to influence their fellow-men must ever keep their eyes, is the individuality of power and development;" that for this there are two requisites, "freedom, and a variety of situations;" and that from the union of these arise "individual vigour and manifold diversity," which combine themselves in "originality."[18]

Gray claims that this rests on "Mill's notion that each person has within him a quiddity, or unique nature, that is his to realize." Against this alleged assumption, Gray says,

> The identities of persons are cultural artifacts, not natural facts. Each of us comes into the world with an endowment of biological uniqueness, but this becomes personal individuality only by our being initiated into a cultural tradition. We may have needs which our traditions do not satisfy or even recognize, but it makes no sense to suppose that there is in each of us a peculiar essence awaiting

realization. As we know them, our identities are ramshackle and contingent affairs, the upshots of chance as much as choice or endowment, they are complex and often discordant, and their careers often encompass radical or tragic choices in which some possibilities of development are curtailed or closed.[19]

If we are careful to separate Gray's immediate criticism of Mill, that the human individual has no "quiddity," from his own counter-theory, that individuality comes (primarily?) from cultural tradition, we can see that the criticism itself will be telling—at least if Mill holds the quiditty theory. But it is clear from the passage I just quoted from *On Liberty* that Mill does no such thing. He quotes von Humboldt, with approval, speaking of "the end of man" as "the highest and most harmonious *development* of his powers to a complete and consistent whole" (emphasis added). Mill and von Humboldt are clearly indicating that human individuality is an achievement of the individual, something toward which, as he says, they are to direct their "efforts." It is also perfectly consistent with Gray's claim that the materials out of which individuals sculpt their identities are often in the raw state incomplete and discordant.

I say that Gray's criticism of Mill, if it did apply to Mill's view, would indeed be telling, because it seems obvious that human individuals generally do not have quiddities. If they did, it would be very difficult to explain certain familiar phenomena: as that people often find vital decisions to be profoundly difficult either because it is, in spite of everything, unclear which way of life would realize their inner nature or because they find themselves profoundly drawn to different ways of life, not all of which can be realized by one person. If one's nature were really finished and complete from the beginning, this would seem to imply at least two things—clarity, and lack of fundamental inner conflicts—neither of which necessarily exist.

The problem for Thoreau is that his critique of commerce and the division of labor does seem to treat the individual's genius as a quiddity in Gray's sense. For if the individual's unique genius is at the outset indeterminate, then it is perfectly possible—no, inevitable—that the individual's identity is formed as it interacts with the cultural environment. But if that is true, it cannot be taken as certain a priori that following the promptings of the market is necessarily being untrue to one's inner nature. If my genius would equally well be realized by being a lawyer or being a law professor, and the market will not pay me to be a professor, then I will not be living a stunted, thwarted life if I become a lawyer precisely because people *will* pay me to do that. Doing what others want will necessarily be a betrayal of your true self only if your self is finished and complete in a way that is independent of what others want. If, however, the self is formed in interactions with other people, there is no reason why the average person's self cannot fit commercial society perfectly well.[20]

I think that Thoreau probably held the quiddity view, or something very much like it, because, in his own case, it very nearly *was* true. To him, the process of, as I would interpret it, self-development, must have felt like an encounter with a self already formed. From his Harvard commencement address onward, his life reveals a really astonishing psychological consistency. It was clear from early on what he wanted to do with his life. He wanted to observe nature closely and write about it. Writing *A Week on the Concord and Merrimack Rivers*, the book he came to Walden Pond to finish, was a mighty effort to get commercial society to support him in this. When his hopes for *A Week* came crashing down on him, he must have been desperate, but to conclude, as he apparently did, that the mass of men lead lives of quiet desperation was probably an instance of overgeneralizing from one case.

The other way in which Thoreau's critique of commerce could misfire is that it might be wrong in assuming that trade, in itself, yields no benefits with any ethical importance. Is there any way, any way that is ethically significant, in which commerce makes human life better? I would like to point out one such way. It is suggested, albeit indirectly, in an interesting passage in Mark Twain's *Life on the Mississippi*. The passage I have in mind describes the effect on the people of the Mississippi River hamlet of Hannibal, Missouri, of the daily visits of two steamboats, each of them a mere "cheap, gaudy packet" from the upstream or downstream worlds:

> After all these years I can picture that old time to myself now, just as it was then: the white town drowsing in the sunshine of a summer's morning; the streets empty, or nearly so; one or two clerks sitting in front of the Water Street store, with their splint-bottomed chairs tilted back against the wall, chins on breasts, hats slouched over their faces, asleep with shingle-shavings enough around to show what broke them down; a sow and a litter of pigs loafing along the sidewalk, doing a good business in watermelon rinds and seeds . . .

After some hours of this, someone

> lifts up the cry, "S-t-e-a-m-boat acomin'!" and the scene changes! The town drunkard stirs, the clerks wake up, a furious clatter of drays follows, every house and store pours out a contribution, and all in a twinkling the dead town is alive and moving. Drays, carts, men, boys, all go hurrying from many quarters to a

common center, the wharf. Assembled there, the people fasten their eyes upon the coming boat as upon a wonder they are seeing for the first time.[21]

Two facts about Mark Twain's description make it relevant to Thoreau's concerns. First, the packets that visited Hannibal were *commercial* enterprises. They came to town in order to load or unload freight as a part of its being bought or sold between trading partners living in places distant from one another. They carried their passengers as paying guests, and those passengers were themselves often going somewhere for business purposes of their own. Second, in a quite literal way, these humble steamboats brought to the village a deeply Thoreauvian value: namely, wakefulness. The packet's visit electrically jolts the "drowsing" village out of its stupor and into consciousness. Indeed, in Mark Twain's account, the value of wakefulness seems closely connected with another Thoreauvian value, with which Thoreau also connects it: namely, vitality. Before the visit, the humans seem, if anything, less alive than the sow, who is contentedly eating garbage. Their somnolence is a sort of happy, comfortable death. As soon as the boat is sighted, though, the town is "alive and moving." The vortex-like motion has a focus and a destination and, having arrived there, the people come to rest and "fasten their eyes" on the arriving boat. One gets a strong sense that awareness is both the cause and the purpose of the explosion of vitality that we have witnessed here. To fasten one's eyes on something, to be truly alive to it, is the end toward which we strive.

Of course, if this little narrative merely describes a particular commercial enterprise as having these seemingly Thoreauvian effects, that does not yet speak to the issue at hand, which concerns the nature of commerce in general. In an indirect sort of way, however, Twain's narrative does address that issue, since the most plausible explanation of why these two elements—commerce and heightened consciousness—go together in this instance will also indicate a necessary and generic connection between them.

The explanation I have in mind would go more or less like this. As Mark Twain makes rather obvious, the reason these people are running to see the boat and whatever it might spill onto their shore is that, whatever they will find there, it will be *something new*, and it is likely to be new because it is *not from here*. In sharp contrast with the narrow circuit of small-town experience, with its overwhelming, musty odor of familiarity, the boat and its contents represent the outside, the other, the alien. And it is no accident that it is a commercial enterprise that brings the outside into view. Trade links people, and it links them by means of their difference from one another. For the most part, it links them by means of the fact that they have something different to offer one another. A yam farmer on a Pacific island does not trade his product with that of other yam farmers. Rather, the farmer's trading activities bring him into contact with people who produce things that are different from what he produces: with such people as the fisherman, for instance. He will not trade yams for yams but might well for fish. Trade will in that case bring the one who works the soil into some relation with one whose medium is not earth but water.

Having seen this, we can see it is no accident that trade routes, like the Mississippi River waterway, have figured prominently in the history and prehistory of trade and why they have the sort of significance that Mark Twain attributes to this one. The nature of trade includes the fact that it brings together products that are different, and this implies that it brings together producers who are different. It also has a further implication. For various reasons, products that are different will tend to be produced in different places. In salt water one can acquire fish but not yams. For commercial reasons, manufacturing and agriculture will tend to be concentrated in different areas. Precisely because it connects products that are different, then, trade will often be conducted along pathways that connect places and people that are different.

Further, because they connect places and people that differ qualitatively from one another, these pathways will tend to bring new ideas and new experiences along with their trade goods. Such ideas and experiences are just the sort of thing that will *wake people up*, in a sense that is vividly represented by Mark Twain's little narrative: the result will be not merely heightened awareness but heightened activity, including in particular activity that aims at heightened awareness.

We have reason to believe that trade will support the very values that Thoreau would see as offsetting the costs he claims it imposes on most people. Indeed, he might not entirely disagree with this. More than a trace of the same line of reasoning can be detected in the passage in "Sounds" that I quoted in IV.2, the one that contains his curiously Homeric description of the railroad. One of the more relevant and startling comments there, that "commerce is unexpectedly confident and serene, alert, adventurous, and unwearied" (417.23–4), seems to attribute to the influence of trade the same Thoreauvian virtue that I have suggested it has: that of promoting wakefulness. What is still more striking is that he also eloquently describes, in tones of admiration, the very characteristic of commerce that I have suggested brings this wakefulness about: its tendency to bring us into contact with people and places that differ from our own homes and our own selves. Indeed, his own response to the train is much like the reaction of the inmates of Hannibal to the steamboats:

> I am refreshed and expanded when the freight train rattles past me, and I smell the stores which go dispensing their odors all the way from Long Wharf to Lake Champlain, reminding me of foreign parts, of coral reefs, and Indian oceans, and tropical climes, and the extent of the globe. I feel more like a citizen of the world at the sight of the palm-leaf which will cover so many flaxen New England heads the next summer. (417.26–33)

Of course, it is hard to know just how much weight we should attach to the admiration he seems to be expressing here. Despite his critique of commerce, however, he is perfectly capable of recognizing that trade has features that are good and even ones that are good in his terms. His critique, as we have seen, is a sort of deep accounting and is simply part of his general project of grasping the real costs and benefits of things. It leaves him quite free to point out the benefits of a given thing while at the same time taking a position toward it that is fundamentally critical. As to the costs and benefits of trade, he obviously thinks that its benefits do often outweigh its costs, since he voluntarily does a certain amount of trading himself. His position is critical in that he maintains that it is easy to pursue trade too far, beyond the point at which its real returns cease to offset its real costs and that Americans tend to pursue it much too far.

Nonetheless, though these simple observations are enough to show that he may consistently say the things he says in "Sounds," consistency does require him to resist in some way the effects of the argument I have given here. After all, for the sort of critique he is launching, it makes all the difference how great the costs and benefits are. If we could safely assume that trade has no benefits that he would recognize as such, then he need only show that it has costs and his argument is done. But this assumption is one that he does not make, and the conclusion of such an argument—which would be that we should never engage in trade—is also something that he does not believe. What my argument indicates is that not only does trade have benefits, but it seems to promote ends that Thoreau regards as the highest. This raises the possibility that it is something that we ought to pursue further, perhaps much further, than he thinks we should. He needs to have some way to limit the importance of the positive, end-promoting effect that trade actually has.

Here I think it is relevant that, in his comments in "Sounds," he does not seem to draw any ethical conclusions from the favorable comments he makes there about trade. He does acknowledge that trade brings us in touch with faraway places, but perhaps he does not acknowledge a connection between contact with distant things and the Thoreauvian virtue of wakefulness. It is nearby things, after all, that he loves to contemplate, objects like the red and black ants battling among the wood chips from his ax or the loon fleeing the approach of his rowboat. This would seem to be part of the reason why he declares that "it is not worth the while to go round the world to count the cats in Zanzibar" (578.28–9). Maybe he believes that thoughts directed at things that are not present lack phenomenological characteristics that are essential to the state of mind that he calls wakefulness. We can readily imagine any number of reasons why he might think that such thoughts represent an inferior sort of consciousness. If I see a hat woven of palm leaves, my experience of seeing it establishes a sort of contact between me and the object of my perception: the palm leaves. When I then think of the distant island from which the palm leaves come, this also establishes a sort of connection, in this case a connection between me and a faraway place. Intuitively, though, the latter sort of awareness seems to do much less to establish real contact between me and its object. In both cases, my state of mind is in some sense caused (or at least influenced) by a real object, but the causal connection in the latter case is far less direct, has far more intervening links in it, than in the former. It is also less certain. Whatever I am thinking about the faraway place, it seems to be more likely to be wrong than what I seem to see when I look at the hat. My thoughts about the island are largely a matter of my imagination, and can be almost anything I want them to be. On the other hand, the experience I have as I look at the hat is something I simply receive and take as it is. In this way, this sort of consciousness seems less arbitrary than the other one.

However, these very facts—that the thought of the distant object is more remote, based on imagination, and in some sense at least partly arbitrary—suggest that, on Thoreau's own accounting, there is reason to think of them as profoundly important and, indeed, as having a right to be given a privileged status in relation to other sorts of thinking. As we have seen (II.3), Thoreau treats a sort of thinking that is imaginative, and indeed seems to have the character that I am now referring to as a sort of arbitrariness, as a great resource for the creation of wisdom. Precisely because it is the sort of thinking that can envision almost any possibility, it liberates us from claims of necessity that will prevent us from developing as we might and should. He even seems to think that it is characteristic of this sort of thinking, the sort that reveals possibility and defeats necessity, to be directed to distant objects. He asks us to bear in mind that the sun that ripens our beans "illumines at once a system of earths like ours." We must remember, he says what "distant and different beings in the various mansions of the universe are contemplating the same one at the same moment" (330.37–331.1). We should see the sun as not merely illuminating our own crops but as sending rays into situations vastly distant from our own. Only then will its light be truly enlightening.

Note that it is precisely because the distant is likely to be different from what is nearby, to that which is *next to* me, that it is associated with enlightenment. Thoreau's campaign for wakefulness and moral reform requires that we free ourselves from the illusions that prevent us from hearing the voice of the true self. As we've seen, a major component of this virtue would be the sort of thinking that reveals possibility through the use of imagination, often by objects that are not present to and are in fact distant from oneself. This rather simple observation obviously has a profound effect on the basic question we are considering here, concerning the Thoreauvian costs and benefits of commerce. Now we can see the very real possibility that, by bringing the distant and the diverse into a network in which ideas circulate readily, trade might well support—in fact, might be an indispensable condition of—the very sort of enlightenment that he seeks. After all, the experiment in living that Thoreau made immortal in *Walden* did not take place on the shores of some remote alpine tarn. It happened on a spot that was a few minutes away (by train) from Boston, a port city that was in touch with the whole world and was, not coincidentally, the most intellectually sophisticated spot in the entire country, perhaps in the whole western hemisphere.

10. One Problem Solved

In the last section we passed over some ideas that might offer a solution to the problem with which I ended I.1. As you may or may not recall, the problem was this: Thoreau's basic project in *Walden*, of cutting back his participation in the exchange economy so that he could pursue his own genius, was only possible because he was surrounded by a relatively productive economy, and the economy was as productive as it was precisely because people participated in it fully and did not pull back as he did. His idea only seems feasible, according to this line of reasoning, because it has not been enacted. If it were enacted, the system would collapse and the idea would become unfeasible.

Maybe it is obvious now where the mistake in this objection lies: It assumes that the idea, the thing that would become unfeasible, is a universal rule that gives the same advice to everybody. It ignores Thoreau's pluralism. He does not intend his idea as a universal rule, giving the same advice to all. He has actually denied that this is what he means. Not everyone is supposed to follow his advice.

It is possible, though, for this objection to come back in a revised form: Thoreau seems to think that most people, or a really enormous number of people, should follow his advice. The mass of men lead lives of quiet desperation, after all, and his advice is the solution to their problem. But surely, the new objection would say, if most people did this then the system would collapse with the same result as before: the idea would be unfeasible.

I think one fully adequate reply to this objection is suggested by my discussion, in the last section, of the quiddity idea. I am afraid, though, that it is a reply that Henry would not care for. It is that his advice actually does not apply to enormous numbers of people. If the quiddity idea were true, as I have said, it might well be true that most of us could not realize our natures in the marketplace. But it seems more likely that our inner natures are usually more vague and indeterminate than that, and that most people are sufficiently malleable and adaptable to find a place in the marketplace where they will be happier and more fulfilled than if they tried to lead a Thoreauvian life of exchange-avoidance.

If you want evidence for this claim, consider the fact that *Walden* was published well over a century and a half ago, is a very famous and influential book, and yet has not led to a mass exodus from the exchange economy. True, there have been people who quit high-powered conventional jobs and moved to simpler lives, closer to nature. Edward Abbey did that. So did Gary Snyder and Jack Turner. These men all say that they were influenced by Thoreau, so it is even possible that Thoreau, and *Walden*, were part of the reason they did what they did. But these are unusual people, unusual in their preferences and in the vivid intensity of those preferences. Jack Turner lived a life of quiet desperation until he resigned from the University of Illinois and moved to Wyoming. He was right to do so. There are other people who should do something similar. Perhaps you, dear reader, are one of them. So far, we have no evidence that there are so many of these people that the system can't do without their nine-to-five services. It has plenty of volunteers without them. (Thank God!)

Thoreau's theory, it seems to me, can easily get around this objection if we drop one of his ideas. That idea is not a philosophical theory but simply part of his impression of what most people are like. The distinctly philosophical part of his view remains, and is better without it. And, as he already told us on the first page of *Walden*, his philosophy "may do good service to him whom it fits" (325.35–6).

V

Nature

1. Wilderness and Wildness

The core of Thoreau's view of nature is in the famous line from the late essay, "Walking": "in Wildness is the preservation of the World" (239.19–20). Despite its fame, we sometimes hear this line misquoted as "in Wilderness is the preservation of the World." That would be a very different matter. A wilderness is an area, a sector of the world. Wildness is a characteristic, a feature of the world. This simple distinction leads at once to others and, I believe, marks two different ways of thinking about and loving nature. If your love of nature is a love of wilderness, it would mean that what you love is geographical areas that are untouched, "unspoiled" by human beings. This can easily lead to a view like the "deep ecology" of Jack Turner, which in his case includes the idea that there ought to be parts of the world that are undeveloped by human beings.[1] This is in sharp contrast with the policy of the US National Park Service, an approach that Edward Abbey attacked as "industrial tourism."[2] This is the policy that develops pristine wilderness with paved roads and pathways so that millions of people may enjoy the "wilderness" every year, with the inevitable side effect that they trample it, blast automobile exhaust on it, and, as it may be, love it to death. Turner's view is that there should be wildernesses with which human corporate bodies—including the state—have nothing to do.

Love of wildness would not have this implication, since wildness might be—in fact, is—something that is present in the world far outside the boundaries of those sacrosanct wilderness areas. There might be a wild aspect of the world that pervades most of the world, perhaps all of it, including the surroundings in which most people live their lives. In that case, if your love of nature is a love of wildness, it naturally leads to a point of view that, among today's nature writers and poets of nature, I find in Gary Snyder's book of essays, *The Practice of the Wild*. There he discourages us from thinking of humans and their world as separate from wild nature at all. "Wildness is not just 'the preservation of the world,'" he tells us, "it *is* the world." And, "Nature is not a place to visit, it is home."[3] There are no places on earth that are completely untouched by humans. There are places that are remote and difficult to reach, but they are all known by humans and in many cases even named by them. Moreover, this has been the case for a very long time.[4] If this seems counterintuitive to us North Americans, it is because we tend to unconsciously exclude indigenous tribes from the reckoning. They have actually lived in these supposedly pristine places for thousands of years and had to be forcibly dispossessed and removed so that the government could create the illusion of pristine nonhuman nature for the pleasure of tourists.[5] One historian tells us that they also altered the natural environment, sometimes in dramatic ways. It is almost certain that one of the features of the forests of southern New England that was most often mentioned by the earliest European visitors, their park-like appearance, which made it possible to ride for miles without obstructions, was created deliberately by Indians. They burned the underbrush to make the woods more convenient places to hunt game.[6] On what we might call the Snyder, or wildness, view of nature, it is everywhere, or almost everywhere, sometimes more and sometimes less, but always a matter of degree. It might well lead the lover of nature to identify with nature everywhere, including where you are living right now.

Which view of nature is Thoreau's, the Turner/wilderness view or the Snyder/wildness view? I think anyone who seriously grapples with this question needs to admit that there is some ambiguity on this question in Thoreau's writings. He can be quoted—and misquoted, as in the "wildness is the preservation" quote—on both sides of the question.[7] Thoreau is clearly one of the ancestors of the wilderness view and seems to have influenced Turner. But where schools of thought are concerned, ancestry does not necessarily mean membership. Oddly enough, one of the striking features of Henry's writings, viewed as a whole, is how little he does discuss wilderness at all. This is recognized by Turner himself. "If," he tells us, "you study the indexes of the recent scholarly edition of Thoreau's works published by Princeton University Press, you will find that 'wild' and 'wilderness' do not often occur."[8] Today, when the Princeton edition is further on the way to completion than when he wrote this statement, it is still true.

Of course, it is also true that one of the four books that he prepared for publication, *The Maine Woods*, was about his visits to a comparatively pristine wilderness, but I can only find one passage in it where the idea of wilderness moves into the foreground and he discusses wilderness *as* wilderness. It is from his famous description of his ascent of Mt. Ktaadn (as it was spelled at the time).

Oddly enough, he seems to find this aspect of nature, the appearance of being untouched by humans, somewhat repellent:

> It was vast, Titanic, and such as man never inhabits. Some part of the beholder, even some vital part, seems to escape through the loose grating of his ribs as he ascends. He is more lone than you can imagine. There is less of substantial thought and fair understanding in him, than in the plains where men inhabit. His reason is dispersed and shadowy, more thin and subtile, like the air. Vast, Titanic, inhuman Nature has got him at disadvantage, caught him alone, and pilfers him of some of his divine faculty. She does not smile on him as in the plains. She seems to say sternly, why came ye here before your time? This ground is not prepared for you. Is it not enough that I smile in the valleys? I have never made this soil for thy feet, this air for thy breathing, these rocks for thy neighbors. I cannot pity nor fondle thee here, but forever relentlessly drive thee hence to where I *am* kind. Why seek me where I have not called thee, and then complain because you find me but a stepmother? (640.27–641.2)

This is curiously reminiscent of the earlier, pre-romantic conception of wilderness, in which, as historian William Cronon says, it was always "a place to which one came only against one's will, and always in fear and trembling."[9] Some interpreters might think that Thoreau is simply indulging in the Romantic love of "the sublime," an aesthetic experience that always seemed to be spiced with a thrill of terror, but to my ear this passage sounds a very personal note: the landscape encourages him to leave.[10] And the terrain to which it encourages him to retreat—the one that smiles and is kind—sounds very much like the charming and gentle countryside around his beloved Concord. He is telling us in which of the two sorts of terrain he feels at home, and it is not the one that is uncontaminated by the presence of human beings.

In "Walking," the position he considers proper for human beings in the wild as he imagines it, surprisingly enough, is that of a pioneer changing the wild to the tame: "One who pressed forward incessantly and never rested from his labors, who grew fast and made infinite demands on life, would always find himself in a new country or wilderness, and surrounded by the raw material of life. He would be climbing over the prostrate stems of primitive forest trees" (240.36–241.3). He seems to be imagining that this metaphysical pioneer has felled the trees over which he passes. Rather shockingly, he even carries this idea to its politically incorrect, but perhaps logical, conclusion by treating the American farmer's relation to nature as an improvement on that of the Indian: "I think that the farmer displaces the Indian even because he redeems the meadow" and praises the American for transforming the meadow "armed with plough and spade" whereas the Indian had "no better implement... than a clamshell" (243.38–40). Thoreau's interest in wildness is not an interest in wilderness.

The contrary impression, that he is indeed celebrating wilderness, is perhaps due to a misleading impression created by *Walden* itself, which tells us in its very first sentence that during the events he narrates there, he lived "a mile from any neighbor." "But for the most part," he says later, "it is as solitary where I live as on the prairies. It is as much Asia or Africa as New England. I have, as it were, my own sun and moon and stars, and a little world all to myself" (426.10–14). It is necessary to read such passages with care. He is plainly describing an aspect of his site at Walden that he loves, but what aspect is this, exactly? It is that he has the place to himself, that he is as alone in this land as he would be in Africa. It is not that there must be no traces of former human presence in the land. Though he tells us he lived a mile from any neighbor, he also mentions, in a later chapter, the Irish laborers who built their shacks by the shores of Walden, which, oddly enough, places them well under a mile away. Indeed, though it is true that the book has no developed, sustained character other than Henry himself, it is frequently marked by the presence of other human beings. In addition to the Irishmen who had worked on the recently built Fitchburg railroad (the tracks of which run along the western edge of the pond), it is peopled with woodcutters, ice-cutters, the farmer taking a pair of cattle to be sold at Brighton, as well as neighbors, visitors, and former inhabitants. The earliest chapter in the book that has any sustained passages of nature writing is chapter IV, "Sounds," and over half of it is about the sounds that *people* make, most memorably the whistle of the Fitchburg train. Indeed, when one surveys the nature writing in *Walden*, as I did in writing this chapter, one is surprised to see how little of it there is.

It is worth noting that the area around Walden Pond was far more worked over by human beings when he was living there than it is today. While he was living there, the process of development and deforestation in New England was proceeding at a ferocious pace. There are actually a few clues to this effect in the text of *Walden*, as when he casually mentions that he can now see part of a pathway that circles Walden because "a thick wood has just been cut down on the shore" (466.21–2). This was probably no exaggeration. In his day, about 60 percent of New England forest had been cut down and replaced by open fields. (Today, depending on the locality, from 60 to 95 percent is forest once more.) The rather small stand of trees in which he built his cabin, like nearly every other grove left standing in that part of the country, was a woodlot. These lots were used as sources of fuel by the families who owned them, and their fate often was to be cut down. Wood was the petroleum of those days. Much wildlife had been killed or driven off. Thoreau mentions that not only could wildcats, bears, and moose no longer be found "in this vicinity," but even the local deer had been killed off some years earlier (544.35–545.3). Nearly every nook and bower of the land through which he rambled had been transformed or altered by his fellow human beings.[11]

Another source of the impression that Thoreau's main interest is wilderness that is sometimes cited is a very moving entry in his *Journal*, that of March 23, 1856. This is the core of the passage:

> But when I consider that the nobler animals have been exterminated here,— the cougar, the panther, lynx, wolverine, wolf, bear, moose, deer, the beaver, the turkey, etc., etc,—I cannot but feel as if I lived in a tamed and, as it were, emasculated country... Is it not a maimed and imperfect nature I am conversing with? As if I were to study a tribe of Indians that had lost all its warriors... I take infinite pains to know all the phenomena of the spring, for instance, thinking that I have here the entire poem, and then, to my chagrin, I hear that it is but an imperfect copy that I possess and have read, that my ancestors have torn out many of the first leaves and grandest passages, and mutilated it in many places. I should not like to think that some demigod had come before me and picked out some of the best of the stars. I wish to know an entire heaven and an entire earth.

He is likely remembering his reading, about a year earlier, in William Wood's *New England's Prospect* which, published around 1633, is the earliest attempt at a comprehensive account of New England's resources. In an extensive *Journal* entry dated January 24, 1855, Henry had written of the difference between the New England flora and fauna in Wood's account on the one hand and his own environment on the other. These differences included, in addition to the presence in Wood's world of the "nobler animals" Henry listed in 1856, a great luxuriance of plant life, including wild strawberries two inches in circumference, of which one person could gather, Wood tells us, "a bushel in a fore-noon," and trees with trunks attaining a height of twenty or thirty feet before their branches began to spread. The size and number of fish and shellfish was particularly staggering in Wood's day: sturgeons twelve, fourteen, and eighteen feet long, oysters so huge they had to be cut in half before a man could swallow them, alewives (a sort of herring) spawning in the rivers "in such multitudes as is almost incredible," in Wood's words. Even allowing for the possibility that Wood was hyping New England's assets to encourage new immigrants (we know almost nothing about him), we can see that the effect of two hundred years of European-style civilization had been enormous. Little wonder that Henry might pause from his walks through his beloved fields and forests and reflect that the nature that was the center of his life in the 1850s was a "maimed and imperfect one."

What conclusions should we draw from these comments of his? Donald Worster, in his influential and authoritative history of environmental science and ideology, draws a conclusion that seems to me utterly wrongheaded. In discussing the "maimed and imperfect nature" entry from 1856, he comments,

> The most important and most poignant purpose of Thoreau's ecological study was historical: to reconstruct "the actual conditions of the place where we dwell, [as it appeared] three centuries ago," before the coming of the white man to America.[12]

Worster, unless I misunderstand him, takes the "maimed and imperfect nature" comment to contain the key to the very point and purpose of Thoreau's nature studies. Thoreau is trying to reconstruct the state of his natural environment as it was before being contaminated by European invaders. As a matter of fact, if we look at the context of the "actual conditions" passage from which he has just quoted, a *Journal* entry for January 29, 1856, we see that it means almost the opposite of this. Here is a look at the context of this quotation. Having just spoken of finding traces of old mill works in streams and brooks he investigates, he says this:

> These relics of a more primitive period are still frequent in our midst. Such, too, probably, has been the history of the most thickly settled and cleared countries of Europe. The saw-miller is neighbor and successor to the Indian.
>
> It is observable that not only the moose and the wolf disappear before the civilized man, but even many species of insects, such as the black fly and the almost microscopic "No-see-em." How imperfect a notion have we commonly of what was the actual condition of the place where we dwell, three centuries ago!

He is saying that an observant person can glean hints and impressions of the distant past wherever one lives but that with the sort of data at his disposal these can be no more than hints and impressions. Surely he is correct about this. And this implies that it would be a waste of effort for him to attempt anything that could seriously be called a "reconstruction" of this ancient world. Further, there is nothing in the vast expanse of the final decade of the *Journal* that could possibly be interpreted as such a reconstruction. In the larger context of the *Journal*, the "maimed and imperfect nature" entry and the earlier note on Wood's book reflect a passing mood. Reading Wood, he stepped back for a moment in which he saw his nature as maimed and imperfect—an insight that in some sense is certainly true—and then happily returned to his treks about the countryside.

I realize that I need to be careful though, to avoid pressing my thesis here too far, or reading too much into that memorable passage about Ktaadn. Thoreau says, in a remark in the "maimed and imperfect nature" entry that I have not quoted yet, "Primitive Nature is the most interesting to me." He loved and was fascinated by wilderness. His three trips to the primeval back country of Maine, chronicled in *The Maine Woods*, obviously meant a great deal to him. The third one (1857), in which he was led by the Penobscot elder and master Indian guide Joe Polis, was remarkably rugged and primitive. Indeed, his love of the primitive helps to explain a feature of his love of nature that might strike some people as odd: his marked interest in swamps. He comments on it in "Walking":

> When, formerly, I have analyzed my partiality for some farm which I had contemplated purchasing, I have frequently found that I was attracted solely by a few square rods of impermeable and unfathomable bog—a natural sink in one corner of it. That was the jewel which dazzled me. (241.6-11)

The explanation I think would be that of the different sorts of terrain in his neighborhood, swampland would have the least to offer a farmer and would consequently be least altered by humans or their domesticated animals. That would be the wildest.

Henry did have a deep and abiding interest in primitive wild places. Indeed, as we will see later (V.4), he wrote an early and eloquent call for wilderness preservation. My point, for the present, is that when Henry talks about nature, when he sings its praises, when he grows poetic and even mystical about it, he is typically not talking about anything that even comes close to being a wilderness, and that no careful reading of the text will suggest he is. Nor indeed does he usually seem to wish he were in a wilderness. Further, he is very interested in the human aspect of this landscape, in the work of his fellows.[13]

What difference does it make which conception of nature we accept: the wildness view or the wilderness one? Please keep in mind that what we are discussing here is not nature as an object of science, as a subject that one may either take up or drop as the spirit moves one: It is something that is personally very important to one's life. This means that the question of which conception of nature one adopts is not a scientific question but an existential one. It is really a question about what sort of life one will live. It is really a question of what it is that ought to matter in the way that nature matters. If one loves nature, these two conceptions of nature make a difference regarding the nature of that love and the effect it has on one's life.

And what difference is that, exactly? Well, a full answer to this question would probably require an entire book unto itself, but I can think of one way in which these two conceptions differ that might be very much to the point. It is one that might seem trivial at first, but I think it is important.

Turner goes some way toward making the relevant contrast himself. For him, the value of nature consists in a certain human experience, one which nature makes possible: this is "the wilderness experience." The precise nature of the value he finds in the wilderness experience he draws from the first sentence of "Walking," which is: "I wish to speak a word for Nature, for absolute Freedom and Wildness, as contrasted with a freedom and culture merely civil,—to regard man as an inhabitant, or a part and parcel of Nature, rather than a member of society" (225.2–5). The value of the wilderness experience is that it enables us to see ourselves as "part and parcel of nature," and in Turner's view, "for most of us" this is only possible in a "big, wild wilderness."[14] So far, this sounds very Thoreauvian. What are our prospects for having this experience? Here the tone departs markedly from that of Thoreau. The picture Turner presents is rather dire. Using the areas protected under the Wilderness Act of 1964 as an indicator of the availability of the wilderness experience to people who live in the lower forty-eight United States, he points out that they are as a general rule surprisingly small. Fully one-third of them cover an area that is roughly 4 miles on a side, an area that can be traversed, he says, in "an easy stroll." Even the largest 4 percent of them cover an area that is roughly only 27 miles on a side, and many are so elongated (covering, for example, the ridge of a mountain range) that a strong walker can cross one in one day. Most of these places are to nature's realm what ruins are to the world of architecture: mere decrepit stubs and remnants. In spatial terms, the wilderness experience available to most Americans is too small, and the same is true in temporal terms as well: for most of us our contact with wilderness is limited to a weekend jaunt or a backpacking trip of several days. Turner finds this simply inadequate. "The further you are from a road," he informs us, "the wilder your experience. Two weeks is the minimum, a month is better."

If realizing that you are part and parcel of nature is as important as Turner thinks it is, this is very bad news for most Americans, who for one reason or another cannot go on extended treks in the backcountry of Nepal, Tibet, or Peru, as Turner has. It is surely even worse, for instance, for lovers of nature who live in England, where the terrain has been worked over by "civilized" people for a long time. And yet, if we think of nature as a pristine place untouched, or at least not touched too much, by human beings this seems quite logical. As a matter of fact, people who work from the wilderness conception might go, in fact have gone, much further. The journalist Bill McKibben has argued, in an influential book, that now that humans are altering global climate, nature has actually ended. It is all contaminated.[15] Nature is dead, and we industrialized and industrializing humans have murdered it. Again, all this is logical if—and it is of course a big "if"—one starts with the conception of nature specified by the wilderness view.

I am sure a case can be made that McKibben's hyperbolic thesis is not forced on one by the wilderness view, but Turner's argument is very plausible, and it also paints a very gloomy picture. The wilderness view seems to doom most of us who love nature to a desperate longing for something that is for the most part beyond our reach, and possibly with a state of chronic anger about one's sense of having lost something indispensable. Is there an alternative for those who love nature?

This, rather obviously, is my point. Of course there is. Consider one of Thoreau's literary models, the Anglican clergyman Gilbert White. He was a devoted amateur naturalist working in England—civilized, worked-over England!—yet his *The Natural History of Selborne*, an account of nature in the countryside around his home, of its flora and fauna (most notably, the birds), and its various natural resources, is also a portrait of a mind that is immersed in the world of nature. I have no doubt that White's experience of nature was more than enough to enable him to see himself as part and parcel of nature, insofar as this was compatible with his Christian belief. Yet Selborne, a village a few miles from Jane Austen's town of Chawton, is not situated in any sort of wilderness. Neither, for that matter, is Thoreau's Concord, and that is of course another case in point. Surely few people have ever felt themselves to be part of nature with such vivid intensity as Henry did. It was possible for him to have a full-bodied experience of nature, and for White as well, because it is possible to see nature as a sector of a world that also contains a human-created sector, a world in which the two sectors interact as parts of a dynamic whole. This is, of course, the wildness view.

To this I suspect that Turner would have a very practical objection: Sure, studying nature in gentle, domesticated terrain like the fields and forests of Selborne or Concord worked very well for White and Thoreau, who were brilliant, even pioneering naturalists. They were able to connect with nature in a vital, even passionate way. But for most people, to achieve anything like that sense of connectedness would need the immersive, overwhelming experience that comes with being palpably cut off from civilization in a big wilderness. To make meaningful contact with nature on the basis of the quiet and unobtrusive sort of nature found around Selborne and Concord would require someone who already has a sort of genius for it, as White and Thoreau obviously did.

I would agree that it would take a genius to do what White and Thoreau did in the way that they did it—more or less alone—but for us that is hardly necessary. After all, people who venture into a primitive, howling wilderness typically do so with a guide (which was actually Turner's profession until he retired some years ago). I would suggest that the best way for most people to get a glimpse of nature as Thoreau and White saw it would be to take a walk through the woods—or prairie, desert, or whatever is available—with a naturalist. I have in mind the sort of person who teaches natural history in a school or in a park or nature preserve. Just as a classical symphony is much more meaningful if you know something about such things as harmony and musical form, so a walk in the woods gains from knowing something about the life histories of the creatures one finds there and the ecological relations between them. Such knowledge transforms one's experience, almost like seeing a flat photograph somehow pop into three dimensions. Connecting with someone who already has this sort of knowledge can be a good way of starting a closer relationship with nature right where you are, without the need for access to wilderness. For that matter, reading *The Natural History of Selborne* or *Walden* can accomplish a similar result.

Even better, for this purpose, is reading a portion of the vast body that is the last decade of Henry's *Journal*, the period in which he works on this document with far greater intensity than ever before. Perusing several hundred pages of this material, in the order in which it was written, is a reading experience like no other. It gives us a good deal of insight into what it might have been like to accompany him on his excursions through the countryside, as friends like Ellery Channing and Daniel Ricketson were able to do. Day after day we follow his comings and goings. His almost-daily trips were typically quite strenuous. Channing was fond of complaining about how rigorous these workouts were. They were often very purposive, and the purpose was not that of "taking exercise" (a practice he claimed to despise and certainly did not need). Typically there was some area—such as a swamp, grove, or pond—that he wanted to explore, or some creature or possibly even a single tree that he wanted to check in on. Often he would combine several objectives in one trip. In the evening he would write in his *Journal*, often from meticulous field notes, an account of the day's travels. In "Walking" he tells us (230.1) that an area of 10 miles' radius around his home is providing him with ample material for a lifetime of experience and observation. Indeed, the area that gets most of his attention is quite a bit smaller than that. The map published in all the volumes of the Princeton edition of the *Journal* presents a square just 5 miles on a side. With the town of Concord near the center, it extends from Fair Haven Bay in the south to the Strawberry Hill in the north and does seem to cover most of the places he describes in the sprawling expanse of the *Journal*'s pages.

In the *Journal* we get an insight as to why he could find in such a small area such an abundance of material: First, his approach to nature is one that might be called "nature appreciation," by analogy with the "art appreciation" we were taught in school.[16] This is a response to nature that involves the intellect—for appreciating a thing requires understanding what it is—and one's senses and emotions as well. It is a response that involves one's entire being. Second, this understanding and appreciation is about individual organisms, their life cycles, and their changes through the seasons, as well as their relations among themselves. This makes one's natural environment, even a subtle, modest, unspectacular and non-overwhelming one like those of Concord and Selborne, into a very dense, complex object for contemplation. Enough for a lifetime.

This is important because, in "Walking," Henry is holding his practice up as a model that we can follow. This means that, when he says that a 10-mile radius is more than enough for him, he is assuring you, dear reader, that you probably live in a place where something very much like this is also true. And this, in turn, makes possible the big difference, the one I have been promising to point out, between the effects that the two conceptions of nature can have on our lives. With the wildness view we have a chance to achieve a portion of the serene connection to nature that we see in the pages of the *Journal* and that Henry recreates by more artful means in *Walden*. With the wilderness view, as I have said, most of us are stuck with despair and chronic anger. Needless to say, anger is a perfectly legitimate response to the destruction of wilderness. But with the wilderness view we are very likely to be stuck with anger and nostalgia as our principal emotional connection with nature. The wildness view opens the possibility of a completely different, far preferable way of connecting, and one that will be available to most of us.

There is an objection to what I have been saying here, really to the argument of this entire section of this book, that some people might be anxious to make: "So far, you have distinguished between two views of what nature is, and argued that one is more convenient or pleasant or advantageous for those for whom the appreciation of nature is an important part of their lives. But you have not argued that this is the true or correct account of what nature is. Perhaps the truth is not convenient."

This objection assumes some form of essentialism: roughly, the idea that when we are discussing the nature of some type of thing, call it x, there is such a thing as a true or correct account of what that thing is. I do not wish to deny essentialism as a theory. In fact, I do not wish to deny that essentialism applies to nature, that there is such a thing as a correct account of what nature is. What I do wish to deny is that in the present context there is a sharp distinction between the true conception of nature and the conception that is convenient (or pleasant or advantageous). After all, as I have said, in the present context we are treating nature not as an object of scientific study but as an object of love and appreciation. The issue is which "nature," of the various conceptions of nature that are available to us, ought to matter to us, personally. This means the issue is really a sub-issue, part and parcel if you will, of the more general issue of what sorts of lives we should be living. And considerations about what is convenient, or pleasant or advantageous, are *directly* relevant to the issue of how we should live. If we were discussing a scientific question, they would be irrelevant, but we are not. The issue here is, in a broad sense of the word, ethical.

That said, there is a conceptual problem. I have distinguished between the wilderness view of nature and the wildness view, argued that the wildness view is Thoreau's view and that it is, in one very crucial way, preferable to the wilderness view of nature. But, aside from this contrast, I have not said what Thoreau's view of nature is. What, for him, is nature? Unless he has a coherent conception of what it is, we may have little reason to listen to what he has to say about it. Does he?

Of course, I believe he does, but in order to see what this conception is, we will need to take another closer look at "Walking."

2. The Nature of Nature

"Walking" is a little masterpiece, nearly on the same level of greatness as *Walden* and "Civil Disobedience," and it carries the discussion of nature a step or two beyond what he had presented in *Walden*. As one of the works that he prepared for publication on his deathbed, it may fairly be said to represent his final views on its subject. It is, however, a rather difficult essay. He issues a warning at the outset: "I wish to make an extreme statement, if so I may make an emphatic one"

(225.5-7). It does indeed contain a number of philosophical thunderclaps. It is appropriate that the subject of this essay is wildness, because this is Thoreau at his wildest. There are some things in it that really seem to defy interpretation. Without claiming that I have plumbed all its depths (far from it!) I present what follows as my attempt to unravel what it has to tell us about nature.

Consider, once again, the all-important first sentence: "I wish to speak a word for Nature, for absolute Freedom and Wildness, as contrasted with a freedom and culture merely civil,—to regard man as an inhabitant, or a part and parcel of Nature, rather than a member of society" (225.2-5). He has made several sweeping statements already. One is that nature, at least as he is using the term here, is wildness. Obviously, I have been assuming that this is his meaning in my discussion of nature in this chapter thus far. He also tells us that nature is freedom—even "absolute freedom." This is a startling statement. Can freedom really be "absolute"? Doesn't civilized life require limits on conduct that make freedom partial and finite? I think part of his answer to this is suggested here already in the first paragraph. He is not proposing to replace civil freedom with absolute freedom and wildness. He only wishes to say "a word" for absolute freedom. "There are enough champions of civilization" (225.7). This means, I think, that he is being a good pluralistic liberal in this essay: the truth about life has a plurality of contrasting aspects, and we need to hear a plurality of voices, each contributing a part of the picture. He needs to present the other side of the case, contrasting with the civilized side, one that the champions of civilization—"the minister, and the school-committee"—might find disturbing.

As he did in *Walden*, he makes it very clear that he is also for a multiplicity of ways of life and is only pleading here for one category of ways of life: "Undoubtedly, all men are not equally fit subjects for civilization; and because the majority, like dogs and sheep, are tame by inherited disposition, this is no reason why the others should have their natures broken that they may be reduced to the same level" (247.7-11).

Though he does say "all good things are wild and free" (246.9), this does not mean that being wild and free is the only thing that makes them good. Indeed, he clearly says that both wildness and civilization are necessary: "I would not have every man nor every part of a man cultivated, any more than I would have every acre of earth cultivated: part will be tillage, but the greater part will be meadow and forest, not only serving an immediate use, but preparing a mold against a distant future, by the annual decay of the vegetation which it supports" (249.14-17). We should notice that he has just said that the wild sector of the world should be the largest. He favors not only wildness but *going* wild: "Give me for my friends and neighbors wild men, not tame ones. The wildness of the savage is but a faint symbol of the awful ferity with which good men and lovers meet" (246.15–18). Ferity is the state of being feral, of a domesticated animal that reverts to the natural. He is saying this happens in friendship and sexual love, and when it does happen it is wilder than "the wildness of the savage."

Clearly, Thoreau's praise of nature is not that of Jean-Jacques Rousseau. He is not saying that nature is good while civilization is corrupting.[17] Both are necessary. But what is this nature, that seems to be in some way even more necessary than civilization?

There is a confusing passage (248–50) in which he speaks of darkness and ignorance as being at least as necessary as light and knowledge. "Not even does the moon shine every night," he says, "but gives place to darkness." Obviously, he associates darkness and ignorance here with nature and the wild. What is confusing is that, in the midst of this discussion, he speaks of the natural/wild side of this dichotomy as if it embodies its own peculiar sort of knowledge: "There are other letters for the child to learn than those which Cadmus [the mythical inventor of the alphabet] invented. The Spaniards have a good term to express this wild and dusky knowledge, *Gramatica parda*, tawny grammar, a kind of mother-wit derived from that same leopard to which I have referred" (249.20–4). The leopard reference is to an earlier comment of his on the way that nature nurtures her children: "Here is this vast, savage, hovering mother of ours, Nature, lying all around, with such beauty, and such affection for her children, as the leopard; and yet we are so early weaned from her breast to society, to that culture which is exclusively an interaction of man on man" (248.21–5).

If this *gramatica parda*—an expression that means something like "the way of the world"—is part of nature, which he seems to have identified with ignorance and darkness, how can it be a kind of knowledge and something we *learn*? Clearly, nature must include, in addition to blank ignorance, a sort of dusky or twilight area between conscious knowledge and mere absence of consciousness. Actually, this could indeed describe the way we do learn the way of the world, not from books but from the world itself and for the most part unconsciously: it is largely something we just "absorb." Once we realize this, we can see that this twilight area does indeed exist. In fact, it is immense. It includes, to take one very important example, the literal sort of grammar: most of our mastery of language itself. As I write this paragraph, I consciously intend to write down each sentence that I do write. Yet I do not consciously think of the meanings of most of the words that I am using. In fact, I would have trouble offering a good dictionary-style definition of some of them if I were asked. Yet I know what they mean perfectly well, despite the duskiness of my knowledge. The consciously held part of our knowledge, insofar as we can make use of it in making our way in the world, rests on a great fund of understanding that is not consciously aware but is present and effective nonetheless. Once we realize this, it makes perfect sense that Thoreau would say that he would not have every man nor every part of a man cultivated.

It certainly is a defensible position to say that the dusky portion of our knowledge, what the philosopher Michael Polanyi called "the tacit dimension,"[18] is vaster than the consciously held portion, and it is obviously true that it is indispensable. Without it, even seemingly simple tasks, from writing a paragraph to tying our shoelaces and even walking across the room, would be impossibly complicated. Human life as we know it would come crashing down. The uncultivated portion of our knowledge provides a solid foundation for the cultivated part.

There is a comment that Thoreau makes in this essay that might easily be overlooked but which seems to me very suggestive and important. It is this: "We have to be told that the Greeks called the world Κόσμος, Beauty, or Order, but we do not see clearly why they did so, and we esteem it at best only a curious philological fact" (251.27–30). He is thinking here of the traditional Greek dichotomy between Cosmos (the traditional transliteration of Κόσμος) and its opposite, Chaos. Clearly, this is his own conception of the natural order: It is precisely that, an *order*, even a beautiful order. If we combine this idea with his idea that nature is "absolute freedom," we get the idea that nature is a system of parts that interact freely and yet produce order. Nature is a certain sort of order: the sort that emerges from freedom, spontaneous order.

If this sounds terribly nebulous and you need an example of such spontaneous order, it is relevant to remember that, due to his connections with the scientific community, Henry was one of the very first people in America to read Charles Darwin's *Origin of Species*, and that he read is closely and avidly.[19] Darwin's powerful theory of evolution through natural selection is an instance of precisely this view of nature. It depicts the organization of individual organisms into distinct species as an order that arises from the interaction of the organisms themselves. Traits that enable the organisms to survive through the age at which they can reproduce are passed on to their offspring. As new traits appear randomly, an organism's lineage gradually changes and new species arise. Darwin's theory displaced the theory of "special creation," in which God creates each species separately. You might say that special creation is a "top-down" sort of order, in which the order in a system is imposed on the parts that are ordered. Natural selection, like every spontaneous order, is an instance of "bottom-up" order: the order arises from the ordered parts themselves. (I think it is obvious that this idea would be profoundly intuitive to an anarchist like Thoreau.)

Given that his conception of nature is of this spontaneous, bottom-up sort, it is quite appropriate that Henry treats wildness and nature as synonyms. Wild things are the opposite of tame things and domesticated ones. Taming and domesticating are ways in which humans take the plants and animals as raw materials and impose on them human intentions as to what they ought to be: in domestication by altering their genetic makeup and in taming by altering their behavior directly. Wild plants and animals are ones that have not been subjected to these sorts of top-down order.

Gary Snyder has pointed out that, if we look at the matter from this point of view, we can see that large sectors of our lives and our very selves are wild. Our bodies are wild. In fact much of culture and of language are also wild.[20] Most of our emotional lives, including love and sex, are (obviously!) wild. Social practices and linguistic usages are to a large extent unplanned. For the most part they do not arise as a result of top-down ordering. They evolve, arising from the actions of many individual human beings as they interact with one another and pursue their diverse individual purposes.

Thoreau's conception of nature as a self-ordering system is related to another Thoreauvian theme, one that is perhaps more obvious: his tendency to think of nature as, for lack of a better term, tending to do the right thing. Late in his career this tendency took on a rather scientific and technological character. He liked to point out point out that people might do well by trying to achieve an objective by using methods similar to those by which nature achieves the same result. In a late *Journal* entry (September 24, 1860) he observes that a barren hillside created by a farmer's cutting down a pine grove fifteen years earlier would have yielded a "dense hickory wood" by now "fifteen or twenty feet high at least" if only the farmer had kept the cattle out and refrained from mowing down the volunteer saplings there. In the late essay "The Succession of Forest Trees," in which he reports his research on the ways forests evolve as different species of trees prepare the environment for succeeding species, he suggests that farmers use a similar method, using certain species as "nurse plants" protecting young oaks (435.16–19). Commenting on a writer who recommends storing nuts in a certain way (which, Henry points out, resembles the way squirrels preserve them by burying them), he comments:

Here, again, he is stealing Nature's "thunder." How can a poor mortal do otherwise? for it is she that finds fingers to steal with, and the treasure to be stolen. In the planting of the seeds of most trees, the best gardeners do no more than follow Nature, though they may not know it. (438.20–4)

This same idea, the conception of nature as a self-ordering system, also enables us to see that there is not necessarily any contradiction in the rather shocking comment, which we saw earlier, about how the American farmer represents an advance on the Native American one. The appearance of contradiction is due to our assumption that the native farmer disturbs nature less, and less permanently, and that Thoreau would think that this makes the native one superior. He certainly does not think this in every case. Actually, if we suppose that nature is a system of spontaneous order, then the metaphor of human life as a sort of pioneering is profoundly appropriate. A spontaneous order is one that is not the result of consciousness and intention. This would mean that all intentional human action and every act of invention and discovery is an undertaking to amend nature somehow. It is an attempt to either add something to it or, in many cases, to replace it with something. In the latter instances, as in Henry's attempt in *Walden* to make "the earth say beans instead of grass," it is an undertaking to replace the unintentional with the intentional, the unconscious with the conscious. This is obviously not a bad thing *per se*. Whether it is a good thing depends on what the amendment is and what it is amending. There would, however, be a caveat implied in Thoreau's conception of nature. It would be, not that amending nature is wrong (he wasn't satisfied, after all, with letting the soil of the Walden woods "say grass"), but that it should be done with the awareness that the unconscious, unintentional, unplanned sector of life and the world is and ought to be by far the larger, and that it is very, very imperfectly understood by us. Intentional action and consciousness float on their opposite like a boat on a vast sea. Or, to take a metaphor that might be more to Henry's liking and more to the point: it rests on it and relies on it, as a planted field rests on the earth and relies on its natural processes of growth and decay, which provide the mold from which it draws its life.

3. The Sacred Neighbor

The natural aspect of the landscape around Henry's home town, and nature in general, have a very special status for him. But in what way is nature special, and why?

These are questions that he never quite answers directly, but he makes a great many comments in which answers are hinted at. This one, in *Walden*, strikes a very personal note:

> Yet I experienced sometimes that the most sweet and tender, the most innocent and encouraging society may be found in any natural object, even for the poor misanthrope and most melancholy man. There can be no very black melancholy to him who lives in the midst of Nature and has his senses still ... While I enjoy the friendship of the seasons I trust that nothing can make life a burden to me. The gentle rain which waters my beans and keeps me in the house today is not drear and melancholy, but good for me too. (426.26–37)

His relationship with nature is a personal one. Of course, the same would be true of my relationship with someone I hate. Hatred, too, is personal. But here the relationship is personal in a positive way. Henry enjoys the friendship of the seasons. This friendly presence is sustaining, it raises the level of his vitality. To attribute to the nonhuman universe a friendly and supportive sort of power is to speak of it in just the way that religious people speak of God.

At the beginning of "Walking," after he gives his rather fanciful etymology of "saunter," in which it comes from a word for certain Medieval vagrants who seek alms by claiming to be pilgrims on their way to the Holy Land (*à la Sainte Terre*), he says, "For every walk is a sort of crusade, preached by some Peter the Hermit in us, to go forth and reconquer this Holy Land from the hands of the Infidels" (225.29–31). He never says in so many words what this Holy Land is, that the Thoreauvian walker seeks, but surely there is only one possibility: it must be nature, the wild sector of life and the world. This is the terrain that is holy to him, the sacred place he seeks to regain. But why is nature sacred, or holy?

As I have just pointed out, the comment in *Walden* gives the impression that the feature that makes nature seem divine to him is that it supports his vitality. This impression is reinforced by a sweeping statement in "Walking": "Life consists with wildness. The most alive is the wildest. Not yet subdued to man, its presence refreshes him" (240.36–7). This idea is clearly very important to him. Indeed, it is the point of the famous "Wildness is the preservation" statement. I think it is well to consider that statement in the context of the whole paragraph in which it appears:

> The West of which I speak is but another name for the Wild; and what I have been preparing to say is, that in Wildness is the preservation of the World. Every tree sends its fibers forth in search of the Wild. The cities import it at any price. Men plow and sail for it. From the forest and wilderness come the tonics and

barks which brace mankind. Our ancestors were savages. The story of Romulus and Remus being suckled by a wolf is not a meaningless fable. The founders of every state which has risen to eminence have drawn their nourishment and vigor from a similar wild source. It was because the children of the Empire were not suckled by the wolf that they were conquered and displaced by the children of the northern forests who were. (239.18–30)

When the famous statement is quoted out of context, the word "preservation" is somewhat misleading. It sounds static, as if Henry is talking about keeping something in the same state or condition that it already is in. In context, we can see that he is not thinking in terms of states at all, but process. He is treating "the world" as an organic system that can only be "preserved" by something that invigorates, vivifies, braces it. Wildness is depicted as bringing about the "preservation" of the world by empowering it to carry out the processes of life.

We need to recall, here, that Thoreau is working in the context of a culture that is still deeply Christian, in which the divine is thought of as God and God is thought of as The Creator. The divine is the fountainhead of creation. In such a culture, it makes sense to attribute a measure of divinity, or sacredness if you prefer, to things that grant one the gift of life.

At this point, one wants to say, "This is interesting, but, like the metaphor of being suckled by a wolf, it is not very clear what, in literal terms, it is supposed to mean. By what means, in what way, does wildness or nature support vitality?"

I think there are several ideas or themes involved here. If we are to understand them and rationally decide whether to incorporate them into our own thinking and way of life, they need to be untangled.

One strand of ideas is, as I have said, intensely personal. In a major statement in *Walden* about his concept of the neighbor, one that I have already had occasion to quote from, he says,

What do we want most to dwell near to? Not to many men surely, the depot, the post-office, the bar-room, the meeting-house, the school-house, the grocery, Beacon Hill, or the Five Points, where men most congregate, but to the perennial source of our life, whence in all our experience we have found that to issue, as the willow stands near the water and sends out its roots in that direction. This will vary with different natures, but this is the place where a wise man will dig his cellar. (428.21–9)

The image of the willow sending down its roots anticipates the description in "Walking" of the trees sending down their fibers in search of the Wild. Immediately after this passage, he tells of a farmer, taking some cattle to market, who stops on the Walden road and asks Thoreau how he could live there in his little house and give up so many of "the comforts of life." Henry leaves him plodding through the mud to Brighton, "which place he would reach some time in the morning," as Henry turns to go home and to bed (429.29–38). There can be no doubt that the neighbor he most wants to dwell near to is the Walden woods and his beloved Concord Township terrain. For him, this countryside represents the phenomenon of the neighbor raised to the greatest degree, it is the highest degree of vitality-enhancing power. He directly experiences it as possessing this mark of the divine.

This, stripped to its core, is his relationship with nature, where "nature" refers to a portion of the terrain where wildness is relatively dominant—more, for instance, than it is, say, in Concord's Mill Dam shopping district or Boston's Beacon Hill. But we have seen there is another sense of "nature" in Thoreau— Cosmos or spontaneous order. Does he indicate how nature, understood in this sense, supports vitality? I think he does, in an indirect sort of way, though the connection is not easy to see. The connecting link is one of the most difficult ideas in "Walking."

It *is* odd, after all, that he promises in the first sentence to make a case for freedom, even for "absolute" and not merely "civil" freedom—and then the word hardly occurs in the essay after that, and the few times it does do not seem to be to the point. Why? I am sure he would say that this is because, in that essay, he never talks about anything else. The subject of the essay, the title tells us, is walking. As we have seen, the sort of walking he is talking about is a journey into nature, an attempt to retake this Holy Land. That is the positive side of walking. He tells us that it has a negative side as well. He indicates very clearly that the journey toward nature is a journey away from a host of other things. Carrying on the crusade theme, he reminds us that the German word for knight was *Ritter*, rider, and tells us, "The chivalric and heroic spirit which once belonged to the Rider seems now to reside in, or perchance to have subsided into, the Walker—not the Knight, but Walker Errant. He is a sort of fourth estate, outside of Church and State and People" (226.14–18). In the countryside one escapes from "man and his affairs, church and state and school, trade and commerce, and manufactures and agriculture even politics, the most alarming of them all" (230.26–8). He seems especially eager to escape from politics: "I pass from it as from a bean-field into the forest, and it is forgotten" (230.35–6).

What one gets away from in Thoreauvian walking is institutional life in all its forms. The movement toward nature is also a move away from institutions. That is the other side, the negative side, of the value of walking. I suppose it is intuitively obvious how this can mean entering a state of freedom, even "absolute" and not merely "civil" freedom. But there is more than a mere intuition involved here. There is a theory of sorts. In fact it is a theory I have already discussed, though in a rather different context. It indicates the connection between nature, conceived as spontaneous order, and freedom. In addition, it shows why he thinks the link between nature (or perhaps more exactly the move away from institutions) and life is so close that they are virtually the same thing. Recall the important passage in "Civil Disobedience" (205.20–6) that I discussed in II.7, in which he criticizes the "mass of men," the "standing army, and the militia, jailers, constables," who "serve the state ". . . not as men mainly, but as machines, with their bodies." He appears to be thinking that it is because these people act *as* members of an institution—as jailers, constables, and so forth—that they degrade themselves to the level of nonliving things. The reason such action has this peculiar power is that it involves "in most cases no free exercise whatever of the judgment." He is thinking that to be alive, fully alive as a person, is for one's actions to proceed from one's inner nature, from one's own authentic, individual judgment and conscience. To be a functionary of an institution is precisely *not* to act in this way. All institutions are constituted by rules that define the positions of the duties of the various functionaries, thus making the workings of the institution possible. To function as a jail, the jail cannot and will not allow the jailer to act on the basis of his or her own individual judgment as to whether an alleged culprit deserves to be in jail. Rather than judgment, the jailer's conduct has to be controlled by rules. In this way, it is controlled from the outside, top-down, as a machine is controlled by its operator and, ultimately, by the engineers who designed it. Machines are not alive. Living beings are ones whose behavior flows from their own natures and not from the will and preferences of an engineer or external controller. To act as a cog in an institutional machine is necessarily to suffer diminished vitality. This is why the tale of Romulus and Remus, founders of Rome, being suckled by a wolf, is no "meaningless fable." As a civilization develops and the functions of human life are taken over more and more by the functions of institutions, people tend to fall into a state of decadence. "Our winged thoughts are turned to poultry" (253.19–20), or, as Nietzsche said, "The preponderance of Mandarins never indicates anything good."[21]

As I have said, Thoreau is not Rousseau. A civilization that relied entirely on the authentic, freely exercised judgment of individuals as to whether to rob banks or commit rape or murder would not last long as a civilization. Institutions and the rules that come with them are necessary and inevitable. The main part of the "word" he says in defense of "absolute freedom and wildness" is just what he says about that Roman fable: we still must keep in touch with our pre-institutional selves or lose an essential source of vital energy and power. The point is to stay in touch with it, not to abandon everything else. He takes it as obvious that such abandonment is not a danger: civilization has enough champions.

He is saying that Thoreauvian walking puts us in touch with this pre-institutional source of vitality. This idea is intuitively plausible to any weekend backpacker. He is offering an explanation of the fact that we tend to find immersion in wildness inspiring and invigorating.

But doesn't this very fact suggest a possible objection to his view, at least if he is saying what I think he is saying? Doesn't it mean that the heightened vitality he promises from absolute freedom and wildness is only available from immersion in wilderness? Notice that this is not the same issue as the one I discussed above in V.1. It may well be a tougher one to resolve. There the issue was whether one can have sufficient contact with nature without wilderness. Here, you might say, the issue is the obverse of this, the other side of the same coin. The vitality he promises does not come only from, positively, coming into contact with nature but from, negatively, getting away from institutions and the rules that overlay and even erase the promptings of nature. As Jack Wheeler would surely point out, even in a vigorous trek into a National Forest or the backcountry of a National Park, one often travels on government-maintained paths, with signposts at their intersections and sometimes posted maps with a helpful YOU ARE HERE marked on them. More important, there are Rangers about, who will issue a citation if they catch you breaking one of the rules, rules that are needed to prevent visitors from damaging the natural terrain or, in areas of heavy traffic, trampling it to death. Doesn't getting away from institutions and their requirements require pristine wilderness? And wouldn't it be very difficult for most people to get access to it?

Henry's answer to the first of these two questions would clearly be "no." He makes it very clear in "Walking" that his case for wildness is based on the promise of heightened vitality, and he makes it equally clear that an area with a 10-mile radius from his family's home, in the yellow house on Main Street, is quite sufficient for him—obviously meaning that it is sufficient for the purpose of heightened vitality. How can this be, given that sufficiency for this purpose evidently means somehow getting away from institutions?

Though Henry in his walks did not encounter Rangers or government-posted maps, he did encounter institutional objects that are even more constricting: property lines and fences built to mark them. How in the face of such obstructions do his walks give him access to absolute freedom and wildness?

I think he does offer an explanation of sorts, but it is easy to miss because rather than giving an abstract account of it, he *shows* it to us.

Early in the essay he does mention fences and lets us know that he does not like them: "Nowadays almost all man's improvements, so called, ... simply deform the landscape, and make it more and more tame and cheap. A people who would begin by burning the fences and let the forest stand!" (230.4–8). That *is* the problem, isn't it? Fences make the terrain tame—the opposite of wild. But is he really saying that the solution is to burn down the fences? I am sure many of his readers have had precisely that thought (I know I have!). But immediately, in a startling reversal, he seems to say that burning the fences is not necessary: "I saw the fences half consumed, their ends lost in the middle of the prairie." Without being burned, the fences, it seems, are already fading away. He turns from this vision of disappearing fences to a vision of the farmer standing before him, "some worldly miser with a surveyor looking after his bounds, while heaven had taken place around him, and he did not see the angels going to and fro, but was looking for an old post-hole in the midst of paradise" (230.8–13). I have no doubt Henry is conveying an experience he actually had, possibly many times. He was, as you know, a surveyor, and he must have often worked closely with clients in the field, sometimes feeling widely separated from them by what the two of them saw, were able to see. He follows this vision with a shockingly different one:

> I looked again, and saw him standing in the middle of a boggy Stygian fen, surrounded by devils, and he had found his bounds without a doubt, three little stones, where a stake had been driven, and looking nearer, I saw that the Prince of Darkness was his surveyor. (230.13–17)

So what is the farmer's situation: surrounded by devils or by angels? Obviously both visions involve seeing aspects of the situation that Thoreau thinks are real: not that there are literal angels and demons here but that the situation has both paradisaical and infernal aspects.

The most obvious theme of this complex and startling passage is that of shifting and clashing perspectives. I count four of them. First, Henry sees the fences as fading away. But at the same time, the worldly miser sees only fences and the scars they make ("an old post-hole"). Then there is Henry's vision of angels coming and going. It is connected with the first perspective, perhaps identical to it: perhaps the no-fences version of the world *is* the vision of the world as paradise. Finally, there is Henry's version of the miser's word, populated by ghastly devils and the Prince of Darkness himself.

What is the point of this little allegory? If Thoreau is not saying that we should burn the fences down, is he saying that we should just look at the world as if there were none? I think we get the answer to this question near the end of the essay, where there is an eerily fanciful couple of paragraphs (252.13–253.8) that are quite baffling unless you see them as an indirect sort of answer to this very question. It begins matter-of-factly enough. He took a walk the other day, he says, on Spaulding's farm. He saw the light of the setting sun streaming through the trees: "Its golden rays straggled into the aisles of the wood as into some noble hall." Immediately this simile of the woods being like a noble hall becomes something more elaborate: "I was impressed as if some ancient and altogether admirable and shining family had settled there in that part of the land called Concord, unknown to me—to whom the sun was servant—who had not gone into society in the village—who had not been called on." Almost immediately, he is describing this shining family as being as real as you or I, though their realm curiously overlaps that of Spaulding: "I saw their park, their pleasure-ground, beyond through the wood, in Spaulding's cranberry-meadow." The trees grow through their house. The pines form its gables. For a moment Henry is not quite sure of what he is beholding: perhaps he hears stifled laughter. But then he seems to behold both realms at once: "The farmer's cart-path, which leads directly through their hall, does not in the least put them out, as the muddy bottom of a pool is sometimes seen through the reflected skies." He concludes by saying that these inhabitants tend to fade from his memory unless he takes a "long and serious effort" to recollect his "best thoughts," an effort that does enable him to "become again aware of their cohabitancy."

What is he trying to tell us here? One thing, I think, is obvious: this luminous family is the wild nature all around him, even in the farm of the prosaic Spaulding (no doubt a fictional stand-in for Everyman).[22] Another thing that is quite clear is that he sees both of these realms. But this is more than mere double vision: the two realms are presented as ordered. If we suppose that the double image of the reflected sky and the mud bottom is analogous to his act of seeing, then the realm of Spaulding—which "does not in the least" put the other cohabitants out—is the one that he looks through, to see the more fundamental realm beneath. The impression of fundamentality is reinforced by the ecstatic account of a recent sunset that ends the essay:

> It was such a light as we could not have imagined a moment before, and the air also was so warm and serene that nothing was wanting to make a paradise of that meadow. When we reflected that this was not a solitary phenomenon, never

to happen again, but that it would happen forever and ever, an infinite number of evenings, and cheer and reassure the latest child that walked there, it was more glorious still. (255.7-13)

The glory of the event is enhanced by the fact that it would happen forever and ever. Having invested wildness with one feature of the divine earlier in the essay, that of being a creator, he concludes by giving it another mark of divinity: that of being eternal.

Clearly, the ideas he is presenting here are very important to him. It might strain the reader's belief that he would leave the reader to decode and interpret his words, as I have, or miss the theoretical point. But I am not saying that he expects the reader to get his point as a matter of theoretical assent. What I say is this: attentive readers, as they follow his eloquent and highly literary presentation, will—at least as a matter of sympathetic understanding—see things as he sees them. We can see the human property lines and the civilization that they make possible and, underlying them, the vast natural order that supports them. We see both the World and its Preservation. Moreover, we get a brief but vivid glimpse of what it is like to appreciate that natural order both as sustaining the human overlay and as far more permanent. Seeing and appreciating is really the point, not agreement in theory.

What the attentive reader gets is a phenomenology of the Thoreauvian walker, an account of what it is like to be such a person. More exactly, it describes the world as the walker experiences it. It is actually two worlds, one superimposed on the other. The walker experiences the one characterized by spontaneous order as the permanent and sustaining one. Thoreau describes the cohabitant family as alien—they have "never heard of Spaulding, and do not know that he is their neighbor" (252.30-1)—and yet at the same time awareness of them is enlivening. The process of cultivating our own wildness lies in fostering this enlivening awareness. For Henry, and for us if we follow him, it is enlivening in part because it dominates and neutralizes the awareness of the institutional gridwork that we have superimposed on the natural realm.

This experience of nature as eclipsing the realm of institutions is one that Henry has depicted before, in an earlier essay. It happened at the very end of the central section, the narrative section, of "Civil Disobedience." He has just told us of his night in prison, of the experience of seeing the town's institutions from the inside and of how the experience alienated him from his fellow citizens and people he had thought of as neighbors. Then he is released, and soon he assumes his traditional role as captain of the huckleberry-picking expedition:

When I was let out the next morning, I proceeded to finish my errand, and, having put on my mended shoe, joined a huckleberry party, who were impatient to put themselves under my conduct; and in half an hour—for the horse was soon tackled—was in the midst of a huckleberry field, on one of our highest hills, two miles off, *and then the State was nowhere to be seen.* (219.23-9. Emphasis added)

4. Environmental Policy

Thoreau was indisputably a precursor of the modern environmental movement. Conservationists, preservationists, and environmentalists consider him one of their prophets, perhaps the first true one, and do him reverence. This naturally raises the question of what his views on environmental policy were and how they might be related to the later ideas that he helped to inspire. This might sound like an odd thing to wonder about but, as I say, ancestry is not membership per se. Marx was not a Bolshevik, and it is at least debatable whether Jesus of Nazareth would have considered himself a Christian. In addition, there are many, many differences of policy among these later views. Was Thoreau an environmentalist, and, if so, of what sort?

This question is not quite as easy to answer as you might think. His explicit statements about environmental policy are almost nonexistent. Time and again he tells us of the destruction of nature by humans—in *Walden* he angrily reports that the railroad has cut down the forests on Walden's shore to make "sleepers" (railroad ties) for its tracks (476.14-15), and he tells us with sadness that "all the Indian huckleberry hills are stripped, all the cranberry meadows are raked into the city" (414.38-415.15)—yet just as one of us might say, "There ought to be a law!," he simply moves on to another subject. Even in "Walking," where he presents us with a frightening vision of the "evil day" to come, when the landscape "will be partitioned off into so-called pleasure grounds," and all of it is owned by somebody or other, when "when fences shall be multiplied, and man traps and other engines invented to confine men to the public road, and walking over the surface of God's earth shall be construed to mean trespassing on some gentleman's grounds"—he still does not call on state policy to delay or abolish that day (233.23-32). Rather, he advises us to "improve our opportunities"— meaning us as individuals, on our own—before it arrives.

Maybe his hesitating to suggest policy solutions to the problems he sees lies in the fact that governmental regulatory policies always mean coercing someone to behave differently than they would if left to their own preferences.

Henry, who told us in *Walden*, "I love a broad margin to my life" (411.19–20), favored freedom for others as well as for himself and was very wary about coercing people or advocating coercion, certainly far more wary than the typical environmentalist is today.

There is, however, one place where he clearly is proposing a policy that is very much to the point. It is particularly decisive as it is in *The Maine Woods*, one of the works he was readying for the press as he lay dying, and so brings with it an impressive sort of finality. I think it does, however, require some careful reading to understand exactly what he is proposing. The main, explicitly policy-related statement goes like this:

> Why should not we, who have renounced the king's authority, have our national preserves, where no villages need be destroyed, in which the bear and panther, and some even of the hunter race, may still exist, and not be "civilized off the face of the earth," ... not for idle sport or food, but for inspiration and our own true re-creation? or shall we, like the villains, grub them all up, poaching on our own national domains? (712.19–28)

What is he advocating? His most recent biographer believes he is endorsing an idea that she calls "the commons," by which she means land to which everyone has access, and thus (as she understands it) he is endorsing the sort of policy pursued in the century after his death by the mainstream of the environmental movement, which led to such institutional structures as the US National Park system.[23] I think a brief look at the context of the above statement reveals something more interesting and, in a way, more radical than that.

It occurs at the end of the chapter "Chesuncook," his account of his second trip to the deep woods of Maine. It comes at the end of a long passage (708.19–712.28) in which he reflects on his return home from his woodland expedition, and on the two broadly different types of terrain he has traversed: they include "wild forest which once occupied our oldest townships, and the tame one which I find there to-day" (708.21–2). There is the woods of Maine and the woods of Concord. Contained in the tame is all the terrain that the "civilized man" finds congenial: "the perfection of parks and groves, gardens, arbors, paths, vistas, and landscapes" (711.33–5). It is terrain that includes nature, but nature tamed, with the dead and fallen trees removed and many other "improvements" introduced for human security and comfort. The civilized man "must at length pine" in the wild sort of land, "like a cultivated plant, which clasps its fibres about a crude and undissolved mass of peat" (711.25–8). Such terrain is too simple and barren for such a person. In his own day, Thoreau sees the tame as invading and gradually obliterating the wild. Eventually, Maine may become what Massachusetts is now. That might seem like an acceptable result if you consider only the "civilized man," but

> there are spirits of a yet more liberal culture, to whom no simplicity is barren ... These remind us, that, not only for strength, but for beauty, the poet must, from time to time, travel the logger's path and the Indian's trail, to drink at some new and more bracing fountain of the Muses, far in the recesses of the wilderness. (712.6–15)

I think it is very clear that turning these magnificent places into parks is precisely not what he is talking about. He quite explicitly places parks, with their sundry improvements on the wild, in the category of the tame, which he argues is the category of the not-enough. There is something more that some people need, and this is what he is advocating.

What we have here is a call for wilderness preservation, perhaps the first one ever published. It comes from someone who believes that a wilderness is not a park and a park is no wilderness. If we wish to understand the full meaning of what he is calling for, it helps to remember that Thoreau's career coincided with the first great surge in the American's westward migration. Two of the most famous events in the early emigrant trails—the Donner Party's becoming stranded in the Sierras, with the resulting winter of hunger and cannibalism, and the arrival of the first Mormon party at Great Salt Lake—happened while he was living at Walden Pond. He makes a few comments in his statement about wilderness preservation that indicate that this migration is really what he has in mind. He says that, as his imagined poet goes into the wild for inspiration and re-creation, "the logger and the pioneer have preceded him, like John the Baptist" (712.1–2). Also, notice that, in the remarks already quoted, the poet will be following "the Indian's trail," and that the "race of the hunter" will be there, along with the bear and the panther. This last comment refers, of course, not to white sport hunters but to indigenous peoples who hunt for their food. A Thoreauvian wilderness preserve would include "wild" Indians! I think what he is saying is that the great westward migration, heroic as it is in certain respects, must not surge everywhere. Some of the land must stay as it is now, circa 1860.

This policy, if carried out scrupulously, would have another implication, one that might easily be overlooked: it would mean that these wild lands would remain unowned, or at least managed as if they were not and could not be owned, as far as this is feasible. That this is what Henry means is reinforced by the vision, in "Walking," of the "the fences half consumed, their ends lost in the middle of the prairie" (230.8–9). Again, land that is unowned (or as if unowned) is quite different from a park, which would be land that is owned, developed, and improved by the community (in most cases, by the state).[24]

Of course, describing it this way makes Thoreau's idea sound like it can no longer have any practical value. In terms of the main thrust of American environmentalism during the century after Thoreau's death, his view represents a path not taken. It is no longer possible for the terrain in the United States to be the way it was in 1860 (except, possibly, for parts of Alaska). But I would say that, even if this last point is true, that does not mean that the idea (or ideal) of a Thoreauvian wilderness has no practical value today. The Wilderness Act of 1964, enacted over a century after his death, was a serious effort in the direction of the sort of preservation Thoreau was calling for. It shows that those who find Thoreau's idea compelling need not give up on adapting it to the current environment. Of course, it might be foolish to expect a democratic government to go very far in this direction. There are reasons, some of which are ethical, why they must do things that are in the interests of the average voter or taxpayer, and Henry has in effect warned us that most people will have little interest in this sort of undertaking. But there are alternatives to governmental action. The Nature Conservancy is a nongovernmental organization that has accumulated a system of more than 1,500 preserves, totaling over nine million acres, and has done so by gift, bequest, purchase, and other noncoercive means (something Henry would surely applaud!).[25]

Once again, we see that Thoreau's ideas, even some of the most radical ones, can still be applied today, though in some cases it might need a little imagination to do so.

Appendix: Analogical Argument

Analogical thinking is very congenial to Thoreau, and to Emerson as well. It is also typical of some of the Chinese sages that Thoreau is fond of quoting, such as Confucius and Mencius. They can be found in abundance on almost any page of *Walden*, taken at random. Some of these analogies are purely ornamental or serve merely to clarify or make more vivid what the author is trying to say, but sometimes the analogy is meant as an argument. It is natural to think of this sort of argumentation as being somehow logically "soft," as lacking in rigor. The fact that Henry likes it is one of the things that are apt to make him seem rather soft-headed. Here I would like to say a little about the nature of analogical reasoning. My point will be that it is often more rigorous, and more rationally convincing, than you might think.

It will perhaps be best to begin with a straightforward example of an analogy, and of one that is clearly meant as an argument. Here is one from an important passage in "Civil Disobedience," one that I have already discussed twice in other contexts (II.7 and V.3). This time, my focus will be on its logic as an argument:

> The mass of men serve the State thus, not as men mainly, but as machines, with their bodies. They are the standing army, and the militia, jailers, constables, *posse comitatus*, &c. In most cases there is no free exercise whatever of the judgment or of the moral sense; but they put themselves on a level with wood and earth and stones, and wooden men can perhaps be manufactured that will serve the purpose as well. Such command no more respect than men of straw, or a lump of dirt. (295.20–26)

Thoreau, we might say, is "drawing an analogy" between humanoid machines (today we can say robots) and human beings who serve the state with uncritical obedience. He is saying, just as machines which otherwise resemble human beings would not deserve our respect, so human beings that serve the state with uncritical obedience do not deserve our respect.

This at once brings out the feature of analogical argument that is most distinctive and at the same time most troublesome. Induction moves from less general statements (call them cases) to more general ones (call them principles), and deduction often goes in the other direction, from principle to case. But analogy seems to reason neither upwards, like induction, nor downwards, like deduction, but sideways. It seems to reason from case to case.

Why this is troublesome can be seen by looking at a typical attempt to explain analogical arguments by representing their unique logical form. Susan Stebbing says that such arguments always have the following form:[1]

X has the properties $p_1, p_2, p_3, \ldots$ and f;
Y has the properties $p_1, p_2, p_3, \ldots$
Therefore, Y also has the property f.

I do not wish to deny that this does state the logical form of arguments of this sort: on some definitions of "logical form," it probably does. I do want to point out, however, that this schema does not indicate why the two premises constitute any reason for believing the conclusion. It gives us no reason to think that it is the logical form *of an argument*.

In case this is not entirely obvious, consider a simple case of a Stebbing-style analogy. Let X and Y be two human beings, and let p_1 be the property "being male," p_2 the property "having a mother named Carmella," p_3 the property "having been born before the election of President Truman," and f the property "having written a dissertation on moral psychology." In that case, the premises and the conclusion can all be true of the same person (as in fact they are of me), but still the two premises are no *evidence* (not even poor evidence) that the conclusion is true. At this point, the most natural thing to say is, "Of course not: it makes all the difference what the properties p_n and f are." That, as a matter of fact, is my point, or very close to it. For it implies that no collection of properties shared by two objects can, simply as such, constitute evidence that some additional property of one of the objects is also shared by the other. Something more must be involved than the two objects and the bare fact that they share properties.

There would be something more involved if, contrary to what I suggested when I first described analogical arguments, there really is a principle at work somewhere in the argument. A closer look at the argument from "Civil Disobedience" suggests that, in that argument, such is indeed the case.

Although he does not state it explicitly, Thoreau does take some pains to show us that there is a principle behind the analogy he draws. He comments that in the most common ways of serving the state there is "no free exercise whatever of the judgment or of the moral sense." This is given as the reason why such conduct does not deserve our respect. Clearly, there is a principle at work here, which would be something equivalent to "Human conduct cannot serve as grounds for respect unless it involves in some way or other the free exercise of judgment or of the moral sense."

Though not stated, this principle does play a role in the argument. The role that it plays, moreover, is not that of unjustified assumption. Henry describes what he takes to be the extreme opposite of respect-worthy human conduct—"earth," "stones," "wooden men"—in order to make this principle vividly plausible. The idea seems to be that "men" made of such materials would not deserve our respect. (Today, we might use the notion of a robot or android to make the same point.) If we search for an explanation for this fact, we will find that all the sensible ones rest at least in part on the free exercise of judgment and moral sense.

What this means is that, while the unstated principle supports what he says in the second case, the principle is *supported by* what he says in the first. But the sort of support involved in the two instances is quite different. The relation between the principle and the second case is deductive. If the free use of these powers constitutes the only grounds for respect, then it necessarily follows that uncritical obedience—which by definition involves their suspension—provides no grounds for respect. On the other hand, the principle is supported by the first case as the conclusion of what Charles Sanders Peirce called a "retroductive" or "abductive" inference.[2] It is supported to the extent that it is a good explanation of the fact that what is said in the first case is true.

This, I suggest, is the actual structure of analogical arguments. The somewhat baffling appearance they have—of arguing from one description of a more or less concrete collection of putative facts, as premise, to another such description, as conclusion—conceals a structure that is a good deal more complex. The first case supports a relatively general putative truth, the principle, by retroduction. The principle in turn supports what is said in second case by deduction. More exactly, the second case is divided into two parts: there is (are) certain claim(s) the author is presently taking for granted (in the present instance, Thoreau's unstated assumption that people who obey the state's request to fight in military adventures like the US conquest of Mexico are not exercising judgment or moral sense), and there is also a claim that functions as a conclusion (in this case, that such people are not worthy of respect). The principle entails this conclusion when combined with the claims that are taken for granted, so that they function as a minor premise. If it is true that free exercise of judgment and moral sense are the only reasons why someone deserves respect, and that people who obey and fight do not exercise these faculties, then it necessarily will be true that they do not deserve respect.

We can now see why, if an argument by analogy is to have logical force, "it makes all the difference what the properties p_n and f are." The p_1-p_n in the first case must be such as will support a principle that can in turn support the second case. If the principle does support the second case in the requisite way, then these properties will also appear in the first case, but the brute fact of resemblance between the cases—the mere sharing of properties p_n, no matter how many such properties there are—is by itself insignificant.[3] The principle, together with its logical relations to the two cases, is what gives p_1-p_n all their evidentiary force.

Once we see the actual logical structure of analogical arguments, we can see that they are indeed respectable arguments. Thoreau's argument seems to me, in particular, a reasonably good one. Both parts of it seem sufficiently cogent to merit a thoughtful response from the people at whom it is aimed. At the same time, we can also see why analogical arguments impress us generally as logically "soft" ones, as arguments that yield probability at best, and not certainty. While it is true that the second part of the argument, on my account, is deductive, and such arguments are at times paradigms of reasoning that demonstrates its conclusion, the first part is retroductive, and arguments of that sort, even good ones, often yield something that falls short of certainty.

Admittedly, this is a deficiency of analogical arguments, but it is not as serious a shortcoming as one might think. Such arguments can be very strong ones—and this is true in particular of the first, softer, part of the argument. I think it is very unlikely, for instance, that the people at whom Thoreau's argument was aimed would attack it by trying to demolish the first part. That is, they probably would not deny that robot-like mechanisms fail to deserve the respect we give to people who are conducting themselves well, nor would they deny that a good enough explanation for this can be found in the fact that such mechanisms do not use (what could be broadly described as) judgment or moral sense. They would be much more likely to attack the deductive part of the argument, by denying the truth of its unstated minor premise. That is, they would most likely deny the unstated assumptions about their own conduct in virtue of which the principle is thought to apply to them. They might claim, for instance, that their obedience and refusal to criticize constitute a moral choice and rest on ideals that are lofty and authentically their own. This is probably their most promising avenue of escape. The retroductive part of it is not the part most likely to suffer a breach.

Thoreau, like many of the philosophical writers from whom he draws inspiration, relies heavily on analogical thinking and argumentation. But this is no reason to dismiss him as a thinker or to avoid taking seriously what he says.

One of the ways in which Thoreau relies on analogy might easily escape our notice because, in a manner of speaking, it lies outside the text: he relies on the reader's analogical thinking. This puts him in an old, literally ancient, literary tradition: that of the fable.

All fables are analogies. They are often analogical *arguments*, ones that, because they are incompletely stated, draw the reader or audience in as an active participant in the construction of the argument. An analogical argument consists of reasoning from one case to another by means of a principle that connects them in a certain way. The body of the fable is the first case. The "moral" is often a partial statement, and sometimes a complete one, of the principle. However, in fables, there is generally only one case given. This, admittedly, makes fables look quite unlike analogies. Whether they are illustrative or argumentative, analogies always involve a comparison between two different cases.

Consider in this connection this fable of Aesop, often called "The North Wind and the Sun."

> Between the North Wind and the Sun, they say, a contest of this sort arose, to wit, which of the two would strip the goatskin from a farmer plodding on his way. The North Wind first began to blow as he does when he blows from Thrace, thinking by sheer force to rob the wearer of his cloak. And yet no more on that account did he, the man, relax his hold; instead he shivered, drew the borders of his garment tight about him every way, and rested with his back against a spur of rock. Then the Sun peeped forth, welcome at first, bringing the man relief from the cold, raw wind. Next, changing, he turned the heat on more, and suddenly the farmer felt too hot and of his own accord threw off the cloak, and so was stripped.
>
> Thus was the North Wind beaten in the contest. And the story means: "Cultivate gentleness, my son; you will get results oftener by persuasion than by the use of force."[4]

Here the first case, obviously, is the narrative portion of the fable, in which both characters try to get the man's cloak off. It includes the North Wind's failed attempt to blow the garment off with brute force and the Sun's success by getting the man to take it off himself. Before saying what the second case might be, I would like to comment briefly on what the intermediary principle is.

Faced with the two very different methods used by the Sun and the North Wind, and our strong impression that the two different results are indeed the sort that these methods would produce, it is very natural to seek an explanation for those results. The explanation would more or less have to be based on the differences between the methods since, except for the results themselves, they are virtually the only information contained in the narrative. Even before the moral rears its patronizing head at the end of the story, the average reader has probably moved in the direction of an explanation: it obviously has something to do with the fact that the North Wind's methods cause the man to cling all the more tightly to the cloak, turning the man's desires and efforts into an increasingly powerful obstacle, while the Sun's methods have the opposite characteristic. Such thoughts would seem to lead us to a principle that in some way or other asserts the general superiority of giving people an incentive to do something themselves over using some sort of physical force to make the action happen.

 These are the sorts of thoughts that an alert sort of reader will have as they read a fable like this one. Toward what sort of conclusion are they supposed to arrive? In a way, I think the answer to this question is obvious. The focus of the Aesopian tale is unrelentingly practical. These little stories are about the problems of life, matters that call for a decision and depend on your choice. You miss the point of the story unless you apply it to the circumstances of your own life. That is, the second case, the one that constitutes the conclusion of this line of analogical reasoning is an account of some aspect of one's circumstances which raises some practical issue or other. Of course, any given reader of any particular fable may never apply the story in this sort of way, but until they have, the story has not achieved its point. This is why I said that a fable is an analogical argument for which the audience is an active participant in its construction.

 This I believe is fundamentally the logic of *Walden* itself though, compared to other fables, it is heavy on "moral" and relatively light on narrative. It is also obviously very complex. There are many aspects of the narrative the author tells that might be analogous in illuminating ways to features of one's own life. Most obviously, these include his relationship with nature, his avoidance of trade (or, more accurately, his attempt to reduce his reliance on it), and his attempt to follow the promptings of his genius.

 To think that *Walden* means that we should all head for the woods and live off the land is to ignore at least two important features of this sort of argument. First, and most obviously, it ignores the fact that the "second case" of the analogy, the conclusion the reader is to reach, is of the reader's own devising. The author tells us that not all of his narrative will indeed have any application to all of his readers. More fundamentally, though, this sort of interpretation fails by being too concrete-bound. It ignores the fact that the author's case is connected with that of the reader by the reader's grasping of the principles involved. What connects the book with my life is not that there are brute similarities between them but that they are covered by the same principles.

I am sure to some people it sounds very odd to speak of "the logic of *Walden*," as I have here. Maybe some of the oddness can be washed out by reflecting for a moment how different this sort of logic is from the logic that is characteristic of mainstream philosophy (which is in the Cartesian tradition I discussed in II.3). For various reasons (one of which I discussed in II.3 and II.4) philosophers today tend to argue for their views in such a way as to impart a certain appearance of necessity to our adopting their belief. As I have pointed out, the ultimate goal, the Holy Grail, toward which these philosophers ever strive is a proof that would make it impossible to disagree.[5] Thoreau's use of the sort of analogical argument that is embodied in fable puts him in a very different tradition. The fabulists (as such writers might be called) do not indulge in the illusion that they can control what you think. But they are nonetheless presenting arguments—in the sense that they are giving reasons or evidence that supports conclusions that they wish you to draw. To the mainstream philosopher it will seem particularly bizarre that the fabulist leaves the particular conclusion up to you, the reader. They are liable to question whether something that has no determinate conclusion could really be called an argument at all. But the fabulists do have something essential in common with the typical philosopher. They do want to influence how you think, and to do so by giving reasons. Rather than compelling you to think just what they think, they are satisfied if they can get your thinking to move in the direction of improvement, helping you to discover for yourself what the destination should be. Hence their arguments, as I have insisted on calling them, are not so much constraining as liberating.

Notes

Preface (Which Is Meant to Be Read)

1 Stanley Cavell, *The Senses of Walden* (Chicago: University of Chicago Press, [1974] 1992), and Philip Cafaro, *Thoreau's Living Ethics: Walden and the Pursuit of Virtue* (Athens: University of Georgia Press, 2004).
2 Ludwig Wittgenstein, *Tractatus Logico-Philosophicus* (New York: Humanities Press, [1921] 1961), 4.1212, 6.521, 6.522, and 7.
3 Martha C. Nussbaum, *Upheavals of Thought: The Intelligence of Emotions* (Cambridge: Cambridge University Press, 2001), 563.
4 Rather late in the process of writing this book, I became aware of another book-length study of Thoreau's philosophy: Rick Anthony Furtak, Jonathan Ellsworth, and James D. Reid, eds, *Thoreau's Importance for Philosophy* (New York: Fordham University Press, 2012). It is a collection of new essays by over a dozen different authors and is well worth the attention of serious students of Thoreau.

I Context: His Life and Times

1 That this is one possible result of the fire debacle is suggested by Laura Dassow Walls in her *Henry David Thoreau: A Life* (Chicago: University of Chicago Press, 2017), 173-4.
2 Notebook entry for September 1, 1842, quoted in Julian Hawthorne, *Nathaniel Hawthorne and His Wife: A Biography* (Boston: Houghton Mifflin, 1884), 291-2.
3 To be painfully exact, the first draft of *Walden*, insofar as it still exists, consists of 119 leaves measuring 9 7/8 by 7 7/8 inches, written on both sides. J. Lyndon Shanley, "A Study of the Making of *Walden*," *Huntington Library Quarterly* 14, no. 2 (1951): 149.
4 The standard account of the arduous process of writing and rewriting *Walden* is J. Lyndon Shanley, *The Making of Walden: With the Text of the First Version* (Chicago: University of Chicago Press, 1957).
5 These details and a good deal more can be found in Walter Harding, *The Days of Henry Thoreau* (New York: Knopf, 1965), 455-66.
6 Harding, *Days*, 440.

7   Franklin Sanborn, in a review of *The Maine Woods*, quoted in Robert F. Sayre, *Thoreau and the American Indians* (Princeton, NJ: Princeton Legacy Library [1977] 2016), 102.
8   Kathryn Schulz, "Pond Scum: Henry David Thoreau's Moral Myopia," *New Yorker*, October 19, 2015, 40–5.
9   Rebecca Solnit, "Mysteries of Thoreau, Unsolved," *Orion* 32, no. 3 (May/June 2013): 18–23. She gives an entertaining series of examples of the comment, some quite silly.
10 Walls, *Thoreau*, 534, n. 40.
11 Harding, *Days*, 177. Harding gives, as the original source for this information, an essay dating from 1901 by Thoreau's friend and early biographer Franklin Sanborn.
12 R. W. B. Leavis, *The American Adam: Innocence, Tragedy, and Tradition in the Nineteenth Century* (Chicago: University of Chicago Press, 1955).
13 Ralph Waldo Emerson, "The Transcendentalist," in *Essays and Lectures*, ed. Joel Porte (New York: Library of America, 1983), 193.
14 Emerson, "Transcendentalist," 195–6.
15 Emerson, "Transcendentalist," 195.

II Politics and the Logic of *Walden*

1   Cavell, *Senses*, 4–6 and 19–20.
2   One hazard of travel writing is that the place to which it transports its readers may not be one that some of them want to visit. If it is not, they may fail to enjoy the book as sheer vulgar entertainment. This might explain Stanley Cavell's comments, which seem as obvious to him as they are baffling to me, that *Walden* is sometimes "boring" and seems "enormously long" (*Senses*, 20). He has a deep appreciation of the ideas he finds in the book, and of the excellence of its style, but the corner of the world to which it transports the reader does not seem to be a place Cavell especially wants to be. Of course, there is nothing wrong with his periodically being bored by the book, but he seems to see this as a fact about the book and not about his reaction to it, and he bases part of his interpretation on this supposed feature of the text. I believe this is a serious mistake.
3   James Boswell, *The Life of Samuel Johnson* (New York: Alfred A. Knopf Everyman's Library, [1791] 1992), 276.
4   Perhaps I should qualify this statement by adding "when thinking about certain subjects." Philip Cafaro has pointed out to me that when thinking about scientific subjects, such as the succession of forest trees, Thoreau is happy to use scientific conceptions of proof. For him, thinking about how we should live is different.

5 For an interesting discussion of Thoreau's use of paradox, see Joseph J. Moldenhauer, "The Extra-vagant Maneuver: Paradox in Walden," in *Critical Essays on Henry David Thoreau's Walden* (Boston: G. K. Hall, 1988), 96–106. In one respect, Moldenhauer's account is diametrically opposed to the one I have just hinted at here. He claims that Thoreau's paradoxical utterances are part of an attempt to "wrench into line with his own the reader's attitudes toward the self, toward society, toward nature, and toward God" (98). I am saying that Thoreau is trying hard to avoid the coercive sort of relation with the minds of his readers that Moldenhauer is describing.
6 Cavell, *Senses*, 19–20.
7 See, for instance: 366.35–38, 380.11–12 and 19–23, 393.30–33, 412.21–22, 488.2–8, and 495.8–12.
8 For an extended defense of a rather different sort of vitalism, see Tara Smith, *Viable Values: A Study of Life as the Root and Reward of Morality* (Lanham, MD: Rowman & Littlefield, 2000). Thoreau's vitalism bears greater resemblance to the one I attribute to Nietzsche in Lester H. Hunt, *Nietzsche and the Origin of Virtue* (New York: Routledge, 1991), ch. VII.
9 Walter Harding identifies these three people, two of whom, these greatest of the great, are of course now completely forgotten: "William Penn (1644–1718), Quaker reformer and founder of Pennsylvania; John Howard (1726?–90), English prison reformer; and Elizabeth Fry (1780–1845), Quaker prison reformer." *The Variorum Walden and Civil Disobedience* (New York: Washington Square Press, 1968), p. 274.
10 I have discussed the contrast between the "generosity tradition" in ethics and the "compassion tradition" in "Martha Nussbaum on the Emotions," *Ethics* 116, no. 3 (April 2006): 552–77.
11 This point is made very effectively in Philip Cafaro, *Living Ethics*, passim.
12 The current interest in virtue-centered ethics among English-speaking philosophers began with a brilliant paper, "Modern Moral Philosophy," written by Elizabeth Anscombe in the 1950s, reprinted in *Ethics, Religion and Politics, vol. 3 of The Collected Papers of G. E. M. Anscombe* (Minneapolis: University of Minnesota Press, 1987). A more recent, well-executed defense of this point of view is Rosalind Hursthouse, *On Virtue Ethics* (New York: Oxford University Press, 1999).
13 Ralph Waldo Emerson, "Self-Reliance," in *Essays and Lectures*, ed. Joel Porte (New York: Library of America, 1983), 271.7–9.
14 Several of these arguments against the ethical importance of philanthropy will sound strikingly familiar to readers of Nietzsche. The connection is probably no coincidence, since both Thoreau and Nietzsche maintained a lifelong interest in Emerson, beginning at an early and impressionable age.

III Knowing Right from Wrong

1 In this way, Thoreau's genius is like Socrates' *daimonion*, the inner voice that sometimes warns him not to take some contemplated course of action. This is probably not a coincidence. *Genius* is simply the Latin word for δαιμον, the Greek root of Socrates' word for his own inner voice.
2 Richard Weaver puts this objection forcefully. He argues that John Randolph of Roanoke represented a type of individualism that was superior to Thoreau's, despite the fact that Randolph's ideas were consistent with his owning slaves and supporting the "right" of Missouri to be admitted as a slave state. Randolph, he says, was actively participating in the political system, attempting to make things better, while Thoreau was simply separating himself from evil. When Randolph freed his slaves in his will he "made economic provision for them," while on the other hand, "in Thoreau's anti-slavery papers one looks in vain for a single syllable about how or on what the freedmen were to live. The matter for him began and ended with taking a moral stance." Richard Weaver, "Two Types of American Individualism," in *The Southern Essays of Richard M. Weaver*, ed. G. M. Curtis and J. J. Thompson Jr. (Indianapolis: Liberty Press, 1987), 100.
3 Cavell goes disastrously wrong on this issue. In commenting on the fact that Thoreau mentions having taken up residence at Walden Pond on the Fourth of July, he cautions us against seeing any positive connection between *Walden* and *The Declaration of Independence*. Thoreau makes it plain, Cavell points out, that he is not independent at all, either of society or of the state. See Cavell, *Senses*, 7–8 and 82–3. In a way, of course, this is right: Thoreau surely knows that he is not "independent," as Cavell is using that word. I would only point out that, in that sense, the *Declaration* itself was not meant to declare these states "independent" of Great Britain. Thomas Jefferson expected to continue to stand in relations of mutual dependence with that country: that we would need it as a trading partner, a source of ideas, and so forth. The independence he declared was only meant to deny that we would be *subjected* to it. And this is just the sort of independence Thoreau is declaring, both in *Walden* and in "Civil Disobedience"!
4 Another bond between people that Thoreau is eager to embrace is that of citizenship. He tells us, for instance, that he wishes "to speak practically and as a citizen" (204.12). However, his notion of the citizen is not given anything like the elaborate development he bestows on his conception of the neighbor. The most likely reason is that the role of the citizen as he understands it simply *is* that of the neighbor. These two words are meant to be interchangeable. At any rate, I will restrict my attention to his notion of neighborliness here.
5 Cavell masterfully recounts the ways in which *Walden* depicts his relations with nature, and the relations between the parts of his own self, in terms of

neighborliness in *Senses*, 103–8. I am pointing out here that this idea has a similar sort of importance in "Civil Disobedience."

6 It is probably on this basis that Thoreau would respond to Richard Weaver's claim (see n. 2, above), which was that Thoreau's response to slavery is morally deficient in that the only aspects of the situation which it even proposes to remedy are (1) the mere existence of the unjust institution of slavery and (2) Thoreau's own complicity in that injustice. It makes no provision for (3) the problem of the well-being of the slaves after they are freed. Thoreau clearly thinks that, for ethical reasons, (1) and (2) are separable from (3) in precisely the way he has separated them. If one is committing an injustice, what is immediately pressing is that one stop doing it. Problems like (3), which he would regard as matters of expediency, are secondary. One cannot use the fact that one has not yet conveniently solved (3) as a justification for not solving (1) and (2), which is precisely what Weaver's model, John Randolph, did: he kept his slaves until he could give them some land in his will. That is, he forced them to remain slaves as long as he lived.

7 Note that, while he argues that the state should not punish him for rejecting its authority, he also seems to acknowledge that so long as he is on a tax strike, he cannot expect the state to protect him against nongovernmental predators. See, for instance, his comment that he "can afford to refuse allegiance to Massachusetts" until he wants "the protection of Massachusetts to be extended" to him "in some distant Southern port," or until he becomes bent "solely on building up an estate at home by peaceful enterprise" (215.23–26). Also relevant are his comments in *Walden* that the only thing that was ever stolen from his solitary dwelling by the pond was a small volume of Homer which "perhaps was improperly gilded" (460.12) and that during those years he was "never molested by any person but those who represented the State" (459.37–38). He seems to believe that someone who lives as simply as he does is not likely to need the protection of the coercive state.

8 Classic expositions include G. E. Moore, *Principia Ethica* (Cambridge: Cambridge University Press, 1903), and W. D. Ross, *The Right and the Good* (Oxford: Oxford University Press, 1930). More recent defenses include Russ Shafer-Landau, *Moral Realism: A Defense* (Oxford: Oxford University Press, 2005), and Michael Huemer, *Ethical Intuitionism* (Basingstoke, UK: Palgrave Macmillan, 2005).

9 The most obvious way in which this sort of process might work out might be to create a non-state-legal system. This might sound like an oxymoron—what other sort of legal system could there be, besides a state-based one?—but it is arguable that law is a much older and more universal social phenomenon than the institution of the state. For a classic account of legal institutions in a non-state society, see E. Adamson Hoebel, *The Law of Primitive Man* (Harvard, MA: Athenaeum Press, 1954). For an account of the formation of a substantial body of law in non-state system of courts (financed by businessmen who were

anxious to have disputes resolved) during the English Renaissance, see Leon E. Trakman, *The Law Merchant: The Evolution of Commercial Law* (Littleton, CO: F.B. Rothman, 1983). I have argued, in effect, that Thoreau is wrong to suggest that legal systems are dispensable, but this does not mean that he is wrong to suggest that states are dispensable.

10 David S. Reynolds, *John Brown, Abolitionist: The Man Who Killed Slavery, Sparked the Civil War, and Seeded Civil Rights* (New York: Alfred Knopf, 2005), 171–4.

11 John Locke, *Second Treatise of Government*, in *Two Treatises of Government*, ed. Peter Laslett (Cambridge: Cambridge University Press, [1689] 1967).

IV Economy

1 The definition of asceticism I use here is essentially the one that underlies Nietzsche's essay, "What Is the Meaning of Ascetic Ideals?" in *On the Genealogy of Morals*. See *On the Genealogy of Morals and Ecce Homo*, trans. Walter Kaufmann and R. J. Hollingdale (New York: Viking Press, 1954).

2 Harding, *Days*, 49–50.

3 For some reason, attempts to define asceticism are often seriously flawed. For instance, "Asceticism is the doctrine that one ought to deny his desires." Carl Wellman, "Asceticism," in *The Encyclopedia of Philosophy*, ed. Paul Edwards (New York: Macmillan, 1967), 173. Surely, some desires are directed toward the things the ascetic is trying to achieve, such as enlightenment or union with God. Aescetics do not mean to deny those desires. Their doctrine only holds that *some* desires should be denied. Which ones?

4 This view is strikingly similar to Nietzsche's view that there are no intrinsically evil passions but that they become bad as a result of relations into which they enter. See my *Nietzsche*, 70–2.

5 Aristotle, *The Nicomachean Ethics*, trans. H. Rackham (Cambridge: Harvard University Press, 1926), 1118a27–9.

6 Aristotle, *Nicomachean Ethics*, 1118a32–4.

7 Stanley Cavell gives an eloquent account of this aspect of *Walden* in *Senses*, ch. II.

8 Obviously, the idea that one is less alive if one is less conscious is related to the idea that one is less alive if one acts on orders which would conflict with one's own genius. Thoreau probably thinks that such blind acceptance of authority necessarily involves a reduction of one's consciousness.

9 Perhaps I should say that, in his later years, Thoreau's comments about (and personal relations with) Indians lacked the patronizing tone they consistently display in *Walden*. The same is true of his remarks about and relations with the

poor Irish residents of the Concord area. On his later relations with the Irish, see Harding, *Days*, 312–14. One of the things that contributes to making *Walden* unique is that, compared to other literary masterworks, it is the work of a very young man: during most of the time he lived in the woods he was still in his twenties. This is responsible for some of the most charming features of the book but also for some that are not so attractive.

10 For an elaborate discussion of gift-exchange systems and the ways in which they differ from systems of commercial exchange, see Lester H. Hunt, *Character and Culture* (Lanham, MD: Rowman & Littlefield, 1997), ch. VIII.

11 Cavell, *Senses*, p. 87.

12 On this point, Cavell's interpretation is virtually the opposite of mine. He tells us that "what we call the Protestant Ethic, the use of worldly loss and gain to symbolize heavenly standing, appears in *Walden* as some last suffocation of the soul," that Thoreau's use of economic terminology is simply "a brutal mocking of our sense of values." *Senses*, 87 and 88. Cavell is saying that Thoreau's use of such language is *purely* ironic: it is somehow a parody of the things of which he disapproves and not at all a justification of the things he favors. The reading I offer here can be taken as an attempt to refute Cavell's interpretation.

13 See James M. Buchanan's classic defense of this idea, *Cost and Choice* (Chicago: Markham Publishing, 1969).

14 Adam Smith, *The Wealth of Nations, Books I-III* (Harmondsworth, UK: Penguin Books, [1776] 1976), 127.

15 Smith, *Wealth*, 112.

16 For an exposition of these developments and a discussion of the work of some relevant economists, see Buchanan, *Cost*, passim.

17 Wilhelm von Humboldt, *The Limits of State Action*, trans. and ed. J. W. Burrow (Cambridge: Cambridge University Press, [1852] 1969).

18 John Stuart Mill, *On Liberty* (Indianapolis, IN: Hackett, [1859] 1978), 54–5.

19 John Gray, *Liberalisms: Essays in Political Philosophy* (London: Routledge, 1991), 225.

20 Philip Cafaro makes some comments that could be read as an alternative interpretation of Thoreau on this point. He attributes to him the Romantic "focus on *Bildung* or self-culture." This Romantic idea could be understood as the very same notion, that the self is something one develops, which I have attributed to von Humboldt and Mill. Cafaro's reason for understanding Thoreau this way, I take it, is that he believes that self-development is what Thoreau is pursuing throughout the events he narrates in *Walden*. Cafaro, *Living Ethics*, 21–5 and 63–5. I would agree that this is what Thoreau is actually doing in the *Walden* narrative, but to attribute to Thoreau himself the idea that this is what he is doing is to leap beyond the evidence in the text.

21 In Mark Twain, *Mississippi Writings* (New York: Library of America, 1982), 253.16–25 and 254.5–13.

V Nature

1 Jack Turner, *The Abstract Wild* (Tucson: University of Arizona Press, 1996).
2 Edward Abbey, *Desert Solitaire* (New York: Touchstone Books, [1968] 1990), 39–59.
3 Gary Snyder, *The Practice of the Wild* (Berkeley, CA: Counterpoint, 1990), 6 and 7.
4 I suppose we have to except Antarctica and the extreme Arctic from this statement. But such inhospitable frozen wastes are not what exponents of either school of thought are ordinarily referring to when they talk about nature.
5 On the forced removal of native tribes that was part of the creation of the US National Park system, see Mark David Spence, *Dispossessing the Wilderness: Indian Removal and the National Park System* (New York: Oxford University Press, 1999). It also involved the forcible removal of white settlers who in some cases had been there for generations but were now relabeled as criminals. For this story, see Karl Jacoby, *Crimes against Nature: Squatters, Poachers, Thieves, and the Hidden History of American Conservation* (Berkeley: University of California Press, 2001).
6 William Cronon, *Changes on the Land: Indians, Colonists, and the Ecology of New England* (New York: Hill and Wang, [1983] 2003), 47–51.
7 Jack Turner reports seeing the wilderness misquotation in a plaque in a government office: the visitor center at the Point Reyes National Seashore. Turner, *Abstract Wild*, 81.
8 Turner, *Abstract Wild*, 81.
9 William Cronon, "The Trouble with Wilderness; or, Getting Back to the Wrong Nature," in *Uncommon Ground: Toward Reinventing Nature*, ed. William Cronon (New York: W. W. Norton, 1993), 71.
10 Cronon hints at the idea that this is just one more example of the Romantic indulgence in the sublime in "Trouble," 74–5, comparing it to Wordsworth's thrilling description of the waterfall in Switzerland's Simplon Pass in *The Prelude*, Bk. VI, ls. 624–40. But the Wordsworth passage does not contain any hint that the author is recoiling from the scene he describes.
11 The source for the facts mentioned in this paragraph is David R. Foster, *Thoreau's Country: Journey through a Transformed Landscape* (Cambridge, MA: Harvard University Press, 1999), 8–9 and 209–14. This book deserves to be much better known than it is.
12 Donald Worster, *Nature's Economy: A History of Ecological Ideas*, 2nd ed. (Cambridge: Cambridge University Press, 1994), 66.

Notes

13 This is more obvious in the text of his *Journal*. Foster's *Thoreau's Country* consists of the commentary of Foster himself, a land-use historian, together with selected passages from the *Journal*. The point of the selections, often, is to show what a close and interested observer Thoreau was of the human aspect of this human-transformed landscape. One of many passages that might be particularly surprising to readers of *Walden* is a section titled "The Farmer as Hero," 33–42.

14 Turner, *Abstract Wild*, 84. All of this chapter, ch. 6, appropriately titled "In Wildness is the Preservation of the World," is relevant here.

15 Bill McKibben, *The End of Nature* (New York: Random House, 1989).

16 I take the idea of "nature appreciation" from David Pepi, *Thoreau's Method: A Handbook of Nature Study* (Englewood Cliffs, NJ: Prentice Hall, 1985). See especially ch. 1, "Making Nature Satisfy."

17 As Rousseau does say in Jean-Jacques Rousseau, "Discourse on the Sciences and Arts, or The First Discourse," in *'The Discourses' and Other Early Political Writings*, ed. Victor Gourevitch (Cambridge: Cambridge University Press, 1997).

18 Michael Polanyi, *The Tacit Dimension* (Chicago: University of Chicago Press, [1966] 2009).

19 Walls, *Thoreau*, 458–9.

20 Snyder, *Practice*, 16–19.

21 Nietzsche, *Genealogy*, III.24.

22 There is another passage, this one in *Walden*, where he uses the unprepossessing name of Spaulding to convey something like the sense of John Doe or Joe Doakes: "What man but a philosopher would not be ashamed to see his furniture packed in a cart and going up country exposed to the light of heaven and the eyes of men, a beggarly account of empty boxes? That is Spaulding's furniture" (374.23–26).

23 Walls, *Thoreau*, xiii and 422.

24 For this reason, I think it is simply incorrect to use the notion of "the commons" to represent what Thoreau is talking about here, as Walls does (see n.23, above, and associated text). Note that he explicitly includes the commons in his list of tame sorts of terrain. This is because, unlike Walls, he is using the concept of the commons correctly. In legal history, the commons was a certain property status: it was a form of collective property. The commons was a portion of a medieval village that the villagers could use as pasture land. Because it was their property, they could (and presumably did) exclude non-villagers from using it. It was not land that was open to everybody. For a classic collection of discussions of the idea of the commons and its relation to environmental policy, see John A. Baden and Douglas S. Noonan, eds., *Managing the Commons*, 2nd ed. (Bloomington: University of Indiana Press, 1998).

25 "Nature Conservancy (American Organization)," *Encyclopedia Britannica*, last modified February 20, 2009, https://www.britannica.com/topic/Nature-Conservancy.

Appendix: Analogical Argument

1 L. Susan Stebbing, *Thinking to Some Purpose* (Harmondsworth, UK: Penguin Books, 1939), 113.
2 Charles Sanders Peirce, "Abduction and Induction," in *The Philosophy of Peirce*, ed. Justus Buchler (London: Routledge and Kegan Paul, 1940), 150–6.
3 Here I am disagreeing with the position taken by Stebbing: "The force of the argument depends upon the resemblance between X and Y with regard to the *p*'s." I take this to mean that the resemblance, simply as such, is what makes the argument good, as an argument. I am saying that, simply as resemblance, it is worthless. Stebbing, *Thinking*, 113.
4 Aesop, *Babrius and Phaedrus*, ed. and trans. Ben Edwin Perry (Cambridge, MA: Harvard University Press. Loeb Library, 1965), 29. I have altered the translation somewhat.
5 See Robert Nozick, *Philosophical Explanations* (Cambridge, MA: Harvard University Press, 1981), 1–24.

Bibliography

Abbey, Edward. *Desert Solitaire*. New York: Touchstone Books, [1968] 1990.
Aesop. *Babrius and Phaedrus*. Edited and translated by Ben Edwin Perry. Cambridge, MA: Harvard University Press. Loeb Library, 1965.
Anscombe, Elizabeth. "Modern Moral Philosophy," in *Ethics, Religion and Politics*, vol. 3 of *The Collected Papers of G. E. M. Anscombe*. Minneapolis: University of Minnesota Press, 1987.
Aristotle. *The Nicomachean Ethics*. Translated by H. Rackham. Cambridge: Harvard University Press, 1926.
Baden, John A., and Douglas S. Noonan, eds. *Managing the Commons*. 2nd ed. Bloomington: University of Indiana Press, 1998.
Boswell, James. *The Life of Samuel Johnson*. New York: Alfred A. Knopf Everyman's Library, [1791] 1992.
Buchanan, James M. *Cost and Choice*. Chicago: Markham Publishing, 1969.
Cafaro, Philip. *Thoreau's Living Ethics: Walden and the Pursuit of Virtue*. Athens: University of Georgia Press, 2004.
Cavell, Stanley. *The Senses of Walden*. Chicago: University of Chicago Press, [1974] 1992.
Cronon, William. *Changes on the Land: Indians, Colonists, and the Ecology of New England*. New York: Hill and Wang, [1983] 2003.
Cronon, William. "The Trouble with Wilderness; or, Getting Back to the Wrong Nature," pp. 69–90, in *Uncommon Ground: Toward Reinventing Nature*, edited by William Cronon. New York: W. W. Norton, 1993.
Emerson, Ralph Waldo. "Self-Reliance," pp. 259–82, in *Essays and Lectures*, edited by Joel Porte. New York: Library of America, 1983.
Emerson, Ralph Waldo. "The Transcendentalist," pp. 193–209, in *Essays and Lectures*, edited by Joel Porte. New York: Library of America, 1983.
Foster, David R. *Thoreau's Country: Journey through a Transformed Landscape*. Cambridge, MA: Harvard University Press, 1999.
Furtak, Rick Anthony, Jonathan Ellsworth, and James D. Reid, eds. *Thoreau's Importance for Philosophy*. New York: Fordham University Press, 2012.
Gray, John. *Liberalisms: Essays in Political Philosophy*. London: Routledge, 1991.
Harding, Walter. *The Days of Henry Thoreau*. New York: Knopf, 1965.
Harding, Walter. *The Variorum Walden and Civil Disobedience*. New York: Washington Square Press, 1968.
Hawthorne, Julian. *Nathaniel Hawthorne and His Wife: A Biography*. Boston: Houghton Mifflin, 1884.
Hoebel, E. Adamson. *The Law of Primitive Man*. Harvard, MA: Athenaeum Press, 1954.

Huemer, Michael. *Ethical Intuitionism.* Basingstoke, UK: Palgrave Macmillan, 2005.
Humboldt, Wilhelm von. *The Limits of State Action.* Translated and edited by J. W. Burrow. Cambridge: Cambridge University Press, [1852] 1969.
Hunt, Lester H. *Character and Culture.* Lanham, MD: Rowman & Littlefield, 1997.
Hunt, Lester H. "Martha Nussbaum on the Emotions." *Ethics* 116, no. 3 (April 2006): 552–77.
Hunt, Lester H. *Nietzsche and the Origin of Virtue.* New York: Routledge, 1991.
Hursthouse, Rosalind. *On Virtue Ethics.* New York: Oxford University Press, 1999.
Jacoby, Karl. *Crimes against Nature: Squatters, Poachers, Thieves, and the Hidden History of American Conservation.* Berkeley: University of California Press, 2001.
Leavis, R. W. B. *The American Adam: Innocence, Tragedy, and Tradition in the Nineteenth Century.* Chicago: University of Chicago Press, 1955.
Locke, John. *Second Treatise of Government,* in *Two Treatises of Government.* Edited by Peter Laslett, pp. 265–428. Cambridge: Cambridge University Press, [1689] 1967.
McKibben, Bill. *The End of Nature.* New York: Random House, 1989.
Mill, John Stuart. *On Liberty.* Indianapolis, IN: Hackett, [1859] 1978.
Moldenhauer, Joseph J. "The Extra-vagant Maneuver: Paradox in Walden," pp. 96–106, in *Critical Essays on Henry David Thoreau's Walden.* Boston: G. K. Hall, 1988.
Moore, G. E. *Principia Ethica.* Cambridge: Cambridge University Press, 1903.
"Nature Conservancy (American Organization)," *Encyclopedia Britannica.* Last modified February 20, 2009. https://www.britannica.com/topic/Nature-Conservancy.
Nietzsche, Friedrich. *On the Genealogy of Morals and Ecce Homo.* Translated by Walter Kaufmann and R. J. Hollingdale. New York: Viking Press, 1954.
Nozick, Robert. *Philosophical Explanations.* Cambridge, MA: Harvard University Press, 1981.
Nussbaum, Martha C. *Upheavals of Thought: The Intelligence of Emotions.* Cambridge: Cambridge University Press, 2001.
Peirce, Charles Sanders. "Abduction and Induction," pp. 150–6, in *The Philosophy of Peirce,* edited by Justus Buchler. London: Routledge and Kegan Paul, 1940.
Pepi, David. *Thoreau's Method: A Handbook of Nature Study.* Englewood Cliffs, NJ: Prentice Hall, 1985.
Polanyi, Michael. *The Tacit Dimension.* Reprinted with a foreword by Amartya Sen. Chicago: University of Chicago Press, [1966] 2009.
Reynolds, David. *John Brown, Abolitionist: The Man Who Killed Slavery, Sparked the Civil War, and Seeded Civil Rights.* New York: Alfred Knopf, 2005.
Ross, W. D. *The Right and the Good.* Oxford: Oxford University Press, 1930.
Rousseau, Jean-Jacques. "Discourse on the Sciences and Arts, or The First Discourse," pp. 1–28, in *"The Discourses" and Other Early Political Writings,* edited by Victor Gourevitch. Cambridge: Cambridge University Press, 1997.
Sayre, Robert F. *Thoreau and the American Indians.* Princeton, NJ: Princeton Legacy Library, [1977] 2016.

Schulz, Kathryn. "Pond Scum: Henry David Thoreau's Moral Myopia." *New Yorker*, October 19, 2015, 40–5.
Shafer-Landau, Russ. *Moral Realism: A Defense*. Oxford: Oxford University Press, 2005.
Shanley, J. Lyndon. *The Making of Walden: With the Text of the First Version*. Chicago: University of Chicago Press, 1957.
Shanley, J. Lyndon. "A Study of the Making of *Walden*." *Huntington Library Quarterly* 14, no. 2 (1951): 147–70.
Smith, Adam. *The Wealth of Nations, Books I-III*. Harmondsworth, UK: Penguin Books, [1776] 1976.
Smith, Tara. *Viable Values: A Study of Life as the Root and Reward of Morality*. Lanham, MD: Rowman & Littlefield, 2000.
Snyder, Gary. *The Practice of the Wild*. Berkeley, CA: Counterpoint, 1990.
Solnit, Rebecca. "Mysteries of Thoreau, Unsolved." *Orion* 32, no. 3 (May/June 2013): 18–23.
Spence, Mark David. *Dispossessing the Wilderness: Indian Removal and the National Park System*. New York: Oxford University Press, 1999.
Stebbing, L. Susan. *Thinking to Some Purpose*. Harmondsworth, UK: Penguin Books, 1939.
Thoreau, Henry David. "Civil Disobedience," pp. 203–24, in *Collected Essays and Poems*. New York: Literary Classics of the United States, 2001.
Thoreau, Henry David. *The Journal of Henry D. Thoreau: In Fourteen Volumes Bound as Two*. Edited by Bradford Torrey and Francis H. Allen. New York: Dover, 1963.
Thoreau, Henry David. *Journal Volume 3:1848–1851*. Edited by Robert Sattelmeyer, Mark R. Patterson, and William Rossi. Princeton, NJ: Princeton University Press, 1990.
Thoreau, Henry David. *Journal Volume 4:1851–1852*. Edited by Leonard N. Neufeld and Nancy Craig Simmons. Princeton, NJ: Princeton University Press, 1990.
Thoreau, Henry David. "The Last Days of John Brown," pp. 422–8, in *Collected Essays and Poems*. New York: Literary Classics of the United States, 2001.
Thoreau, Henry David. *The Maine Woods*, pp. 589–845, in *A Week on the Concord and Merrimack Rivers, Walden; or, Life in the Woods, The Maine Woods, Cape Cod*. New York: Literary Classics of the United States, 1985.
Thoreau, Henry David. "Martyrdom of John Brown," pp. 418–21, in *Collected Essays and Poems*. New York: Literary Classics of the United States, 2001.
Thoreau, Henry David. "A Plea for Captain John Brown," pp. 396–417, in *Collected Essays and Poems*. New York: Literary Classics of the United States, 2001.
Thoreau, Henry David. "The Succession of Forest Trees," pp. 429–43, in *Collected Essays and Poems*. New York: Literary Classics of the United States, 2001.
Thoreau, Henry David. *Walden*, pp. 321–587, in *A Week on the Concord and Merrimack Rivers, Walden; or, Life in the Woods, The Maine Woods, Cape Cod*. New York: Literary Classics of the United States, 1985.
Thoreau, Henry David. "Walking," pp. 225–55, in *Collected Essays and Poems*. New York: Literary Classics of the United States, 2001.

Thoreau, Henry David. *A Week on the Concord and Merrimack Rivers*, pp. 1–319, in *A Week on the Concord and Merrimack Rivers, Walden; or, Life in the Woods, The Maine Woods, Cape Cod*. New York: Literary Classics of the United States, 1985.

Trakman, Leon E. *The Law Merchant: The Evolution of Commercial Law*. Littleton, CO: F.B. Rothman, 1983.

Turner, Jack. *The Abstract Wild*. Tucson: University of Arizona Press, 1996.

Twain, Mark, "Life on the Mississippi," in *Mississippi Writings*. New York: Library of America, 1982.

Walls, Laura Dassow. *Henry David Thoreau: A Life*. Chicago: University of Chicago Press, 2017.

Weaver, Richard. "Two Types of American Individualism," pp. 77–103, in *The Southern Essays of Richard M. Weaver*, edited By G. M. Curtis and J. J. Thompson Jr. Indianapolis, IN: Liberty Press, 1987.

Wellman, Carl. "Asceticism," p. 173, in *The Encyclopedia of Philosophy*, edited by Paul Edwards. New York: Macmillan, 1967.

Wittgenstein, Ludwig. *Tractatus Logico-Philosophicus*. New York: Humanities Press, [1921] 1961.

Wordsworth, William, "The Prelude," pp. 124–221, in *The Poetical Works of William Wordsworth*. Cambridge edition, revised by Paul D. Sheats. Boston: Houghton Mifflin, 1982.

Worster, Donald. *Nature's Economy: A History of Ecological Ideas*. 2nd ed. Cambridge: Cambridge University Press, 1994.

Index

Abbey, Edward 109, 111
analogical argument
  is based on "retroduction" 143
  contrasted with induction and deduction 141–2
  logical structure of 142–3
anarchy (*see also* neighbor) 16, 62–4
  non-state legal systems 153 n.9
Aristotle x, 39, 41, 75, 85–6
asceticism 77–84, 154 nn.1, 3
  defined 77–8
  includes hostility to trade 79–80
  and the rank order of functions 80–4

Brown, John 71–4

Cafaro, Philip x, xii, 150 n.4, 151 n.11, 155 n.20
Cavell, Stanley x–xi, 31–2, 150 n.2, 152 n.3, 152 n.5, 154 n.7
citizenship *See* neighbor
civilization 123–4, 131–2, 135–6
commerce *See* trade
conscience (*see also* intuitionism *and* genius) 48, 52, 55
Cronon, William 113, 156 n.10

Darwin, Charles 125–6
Disobedience, Civil 15–16, 41, 47–8, 59–71, 73–4
  good in itself 59–61
  part of the political good 61–2
  placing the individual outside the state 62

Emerson, Ralph Waldo 2, 3, 5, 12–13, 33–4, 41, 141, 151 n.14
Emerson, William 3
expediency, the rule of (*see also* utilitarianism) 55–6, 58–9, 62
experiment (*see also* proof) ix, 10, 20–1, 22, 37, 64, 100

fables
  are analogies 145–6
  are liberating 147
  and *Walden* 21, 22, 146–7
Foster, David R. 156 n.11, 157 n.13
freedom, absolute 123, 130–6

genius 33 (*see also* virtue *and* conscience)
  is a guide for conduct 34, 44, 45–6
gift-exchange *See* trade
government *See* state.
Gray, John 101–2

Hawthorne, Nathaniel 4, 10
Humboldt, Wilhem von 101, 102, 155 n.20

Indians 88–9, 112, 113–14, 115, 138, 154 n.9, 156 n.5
intuitionism, ethical 49–71
  intuitionism proper 49, 50, 56, 64, 65–8, 69–70
  methodological intuitionism 49–50, 68–9
  narrow interpretation of 68–71, 73–4
  and the problem of social order 65–8
  supplanting the authority of the state 54, 56

Kant, Immanuel 11–12
Katahdin (Ktaadn) 112–13, 117

Labor, Division of 92–8
  focus of T's critique of commerce 92, 95
  T on the circumspect pursuit of 95–8
Leavis, R. W. B. 10
Locke, John 73–4

McKibben, Bill 119
Mill, John Stuart 101–2, 155 n.20
Moldenhauer, Joseph J. 151 n.5

narrow interpretation, the *See* intuitionism
nature
  an existential argument for the wildness view 117–22
  is sacred or holy 127–36
  is a source of vitality and power 127–36
  is spontaneous order 124–6
  the wilderness view 111
  the wildness view 111–17
natural selection 125–6
neighbor 16–17, 62–4, 74–6, 127–36
  and citizenship 152 n.4
necessity 24–8
  logical 24, 25–28
  vital (necessities of life) 25, 29
Nietzsche, Friedrich 23, 131, 151 n.8, 151 n.14, 154 nn. 1, n. 4
Nussbaum, Martha C. x, 151 n.10

Paley, William 57–9
paradox 16, 23–4, 31, 44, 50, 74, 151 n.5
Peirce, Charles Sanders 143
philanthropy 36–45
pluralism (*see also* vitalism) 35–36, 44–5, 52, 108–9
  an exception to T's 87
possibility *See* proof
proof (*see also* experiment)
  a guide for conduct 32–6
  showing necessity 24
  showing possibility 28–31

responsibility, vicarious 53–4
Rousseau, Jean-Jacques 11, 23, 124, 131

Smith, Adam 92, 95
Smith, Tara 151 n.8
Snyder, Gary 109, 111, 12, 126
Socrates 152 n.1
Solnit, Rebecca 8
state
  actual 16–17
  ideal 15–16
  inimical to the human spirit 47–8
  T has no right to the protection of 153 n.7

Stebbing, L. Susan 142, 158 n.3

terrorist, problem of the 68, 71, 73–4
Thoreau, Cynthia Dunbar 1, 8
Thoreau, Henry David
  "Civil Disobedience" 15–17
  Journal xi, 1, 2, 4, 5, 6, 116–17, 120–21
  Maine Woods, The 6, 7, 112–13
  "Succession of Forest Trees, The" 4, 126–7, 150 n.4
  Walden 5, 6, 17–22, 149 n. 3
    and "Civil Disobedience" 17
  Walking 6, 122
  Week on the Concord and Merrimack Rivers, A 5–6
Thoreau Sr., John 1–2
Thoreau Jr., John 3
trade 78–108
  vs. gift exchange and exchange-avoidance 88–9
  replying to T's critique of 101–8
  T's negative comments about 78–9
  T's positive comments about 80
transcendentalism 11–13
Turner, Jack 109, 111, 112, 118–19, 119–20
Twain, Mark 103–5

utilitarianism 57–9

vegetarianism 37–8, 50–1, 54
virtue
  defined 38
  is following one's genius 34–5, 46–7
  and happiness 59–61
  and wakefulness 85–7
virtue ethics 40–3, 46, 72
vitalism 32–6, 44, 45, 46, 47, 49–50, 51, 68, 75, 87, 98, 104, 128–36

Walls, Laura Dassow 8, 137, 149 n.1, 157 n.24
Weaver, Richard 152 n.2, 153 n.6
Whitman, Walt 3
Wittgenstein, Ludwig x
Worster, Donald 116–17

www.ingramcontent.com/pod-product-compliance
Lightning Source LLC
Chambersburg PA
CBHW052047300426
44117CB00012B/2014